A S I A N

E L E M E N T S

JANE EDWARDS

Photography by
ANDREW WOOD

20.00

INTERIOR DESIGN

ASIA   ORIENTAL DESIGN

conran
OCTOPUS

First published in 1999
by Conran Octopus Limited.
37 Shelton Street
London WC2H 9HN
a part of Octopus Publishing Group

Commissioning editor Suzannah Gough
Managing editor Catriona Woodburn
Editorial assistant Maxine McCaghy
Copy editors Gillian Haslam and Barbara Mellor
Art editor Karen Bowen
Production Oliver Jeffreys

A catalogue record for this book is available from the
British Library

ISBN 1 84091 032 1

Colour origination by Sang Choy International, Singapore
Printed in China

PAGE 1 *Detail of a yin and yang symbol on a canvas door-hanging (noren) in Japan.*
PAGE 2 *At Sun House in Sri Lanka, white unifies and highlights the architectural detail in this hexagonal storage corridor, creating a transitional space between the utilitarian kitchen and opulent dining room.*
PAGE 3 *The imprint of an ink 'chop' (carved printing block) by Chinese artist Way Man Sing in Hong Kong.*

AIR
15

EARTH
43

CONTENTS

6

Right *Traditional Javanese houses, such as this 1930s'
one in Jogjakarta, are built around a central pavilion
called a* pendopo. *The rooms surrounding the* pendopo
*are shadowy and cool, providing respite from sunlight
and heat. Locally-made polished cement floor tiles are
cool to the touch. A window of green stained-glass
triangles, typical of the region, lets in just enough light
to see by. The room is furnished with plain upholstery
and has clear surfaces adding to its refreshing simplicity.
On the wall hang two wood and gilt Chinese calligraphy
signs; the glass bottle was originally used to import and
export liquids to and from Indonesia.*

Following spread *This Bangkok entrance hall, designed
by Christian Liaigre, combines cool modernist elements
with oriental motifs. The monochromatic contrast of
creamy limestone, whitewashed walls and limed oak
with dark wenge wood evokes the restraint of traditional
Chinese interiors. Raw Thai silk lines a cupboard,
allowing air to circulate – an important consideration
in humid climates. An austere high-backed bench by
Liaigre owes its simplicity of form to classic Chinese
furniture, and works well with the 'horseshoe' chairs.*

The creative dialogue between East and West is as old as the trade routes, and opposing cultures have a history of cross-fertilization. Strong links and comparisons can be drawn between the development of modern architecture and the traditional buildings of Asia. Built from what the earth had to offer — mud, clay, straw, wood or stone — Asian buildings evolved organically, reflecting practical needs, social aspirations and religious beliefs. Modern architects share a fascination for what Frank Lloyd Wright described as 'the timeless vernacular' of these traditional dwellings.

Today's Western aesthetic incorporates the best of uncluttered living and technology with a softer modernism, to satisfy our sensual human needs through the inclusion of natural materials and organic forms. These create a tactile, harmonious living environment, reinforcing our connection with nature and adding softness to harder, unyielding surfaces: warm sandstone and smooth teak, for example, set against glass, metal or plastic.

Right *Nature and the elements have historically dictated people's beliefs and customs, art and architecture. In Japan, the cherry blossom season in early April is a time to get riotously drunk under the delicate pink and white blossoms, celebrating the end of winter and the beginning of spring. The fragile flowers are easily destroyed by wind and rain, and usually last only a few days before their confetti-like petals are strewn across the countryside, leaving the trees bare once more. For the Japanese, the fleeting beauty of cherry blossom symbolizes the transience and frailty of all life. The camellia, which flowers through winter and falls whole from the shrub, is also deeply symbolic and traditionally betokens the qualities of the samurai warrior, ever ready to die.*

The interiors featured in this book reflect a timeless pan-Asian aesthetic, incorporating both traditional and contemporary designs. Whether in urban or rural settings, on sprawling estates or in small apartments, they are all unified by an appreciation of uniquely beautiful natural materials; a restrained decorative style; a 'less is more' attitude.

In the West there has been a steadily growing appreciation of individually produced craft objects. Much of the traditional craft and furniture of Asia is imbued with this living, understated beauty: functional, almost minimalist, pared down forms made of natural materials such as coconut wood, lava stone, shell or bone, with designs that allow you to appreciate the beauty of the material as well as the form of the piece. It is true that many craft traditions in Asia are extremely ornate — Thai silver and enamel wares and mother-of-pearl inlay are intricately decorated, while Balinese art and wood carving are as exuberant as the island's tropical landscape. Here, however, we focus on crafts and furniture that share an understated aesthetic, highlighting the essence of the material from which a piece is made, rather than its surface decoration. Highly decorative elements are incorporated at times, but with restraint, allowing the shape of a piece to come through regardless of its ornamentation.

The Japanese concept of *wabi* — the spirit of unostentatious refinement — evolved as a reaction against the opulence and extravagance of the Momoyam culture at the end of the sixteenth century. In rejecting the gilt and glory of decoration of this period of Japanese history, the spirit of *wabi* looked for beauty in coarse, plain materials. *Wabi* is at the heart of much of Japan's distinctive craft traditions, but can be found in anything, anywhere, that resonates with purity and truth. Similarly, Zen Buddhism eschews all things decorative and ostentatious. The most austere and ascetic of all Asian religions, its followers believe in the exclusion of all superficial things. It is to these diverse but related Asian values, beliefs and traditions that we are drawn today in our search for harmony and simplification in our everyday lives.

While the Asian continent is rapidly changing, its daily life is still imbued with a spiritual mysticism, steeped in ancient religions and traditional beliefs: Taoism and Confucianism in China, Shintoism in Japan, and Buddhism and Hinduism — which spread eastwards from India across the whole continent. Seasons, climate and the cycle of life play an important role in all these beliefs. In China and Japan, the start of the new year coincides with the arrival of spring, rather than occurring in the depths of winter, as it does in the West. The ancient Chinese firmly believed that nature is 'the great space', and that heaven, earth and man are one. They saw no conflict in the inclusion of the landscape into the living space for it simply reflected the concept of yin and yang, at the root of much of Asian thought, which reasons that opposite elements are inextricably linked and together create a natural harmony.

Asia assails all the senses with a kaleidoscope of colour and life, a cacophony of discordant sounds in the city, a heady nocturnal thrum in the countryside, and, not least, an almost overwhelming cocktail of strange and exotic scents. Within this turmoil, the home becomes an essential haven of peace, a private sanctuary from the chaos and the hectic pace of the outside world.

Air, the first chapter in this book, focuses on how space and light are used in Asian dwellings, examines the flexible and open organization specific to traditional homes and how light can be harnessed to add to that spatial experience. Storage and lighting ideas are also featured.

Central to the Earth section are gardens and landscapes, and the lack of distinction between inside and outside space which is typical of the Asian home. This chapter also uncovers the diverse use of the earth's materials — mud, clay, stone and concrete — in buildings, decoration and gardens.

Wood looks at things made entirely of wood, from buildings in Thailand that also use wooden pins rather than metal nails to hold them together, to simple carved cooking utensils. This section also features various wood-related organic materials — rattan, hemp and cotton, for example, which, when woven, can create textiles and matting for the home. New, sustainable materials, alternatives to the region's

threatened and previously over-used hardwoods, are vitally important today; and this section considers the fast-growing, plentiful and versatile resources of bamboo, coconut wood, jack wood and palm wood.

In the chapter on Fire we focus on the Asian kitchen and its typical set-up, culinary traditions such as the centuries-old Japanese tea ceremony, and the variety of kitchen equipment and utensils needed to produce the diverse array of Asian cuisine. Tableware and display are also covered, including an overview of ceramic traditions across the continent.

Finally, we explore Water: landscaping with water, its cooling and calming properties when used in the home and the courtyard, swimming pools and bathing. Bathing traditions are a unique and fascinating part of traditional Asian life and bathrooms are correspondingly different.

I was often asked during our four-month photographic trip, 'What is Asian design exactly?' — a question impossible to answer in just a few sentences. In response, I have to say that this book is a personal interpretation of Asia, reflecting the marriage of traditional and contemporary architecture, craft and design that I consider relevant to international design today. I hope that by including six diverse cultures I have succeeded in creating a distillation that is the essence of natural and harmonious Asian style.

Left *A coil of incense gently burning in a Sri Lankan home signifies the transition from daylight to nightfall, creating an atmosphere of peace that closes the house in on itself as evening draws in.*

Above *The owner of this small apartment has created a cool but sensual haven in Bangkok, arguably Asia's most chaotic city. Natural materials in a clean white space soothe both the soul and the mind. The 'temple doors', with their window openings, chunky doorlatch and raised threshold, conceal the owner's walk-in closet, which enables him to keep clutter in the main space to a minimum.*

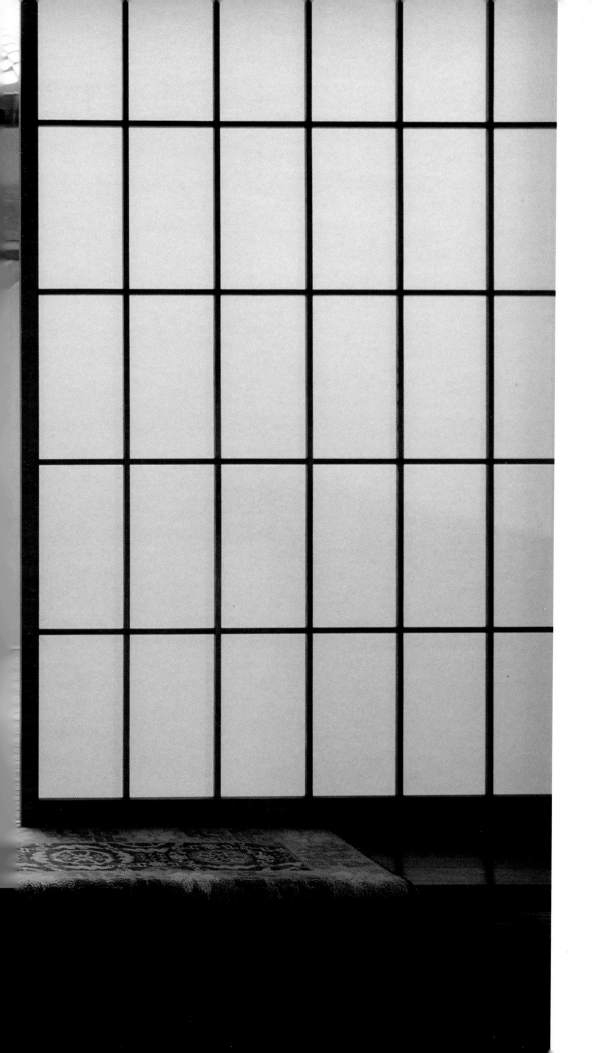

AIR

Previous spread *Airiness and space are the dominant themes in this contemporary house in Kyoto, Japan, designed by Yasui Moko. Pale wood sliding doors, painted with a graphic bamboo design, are viewed from the living area across the courtyard. The perspective is framed by paper shoji screens, enhancing the geometric order of the architecture and emphasizing its spatial depth. Using conventional materials, motifs and layout, the architect has created an interior which is both starkly modern and reassuringly traditional, an appropriate synthesis within the context of Japan's ancient capital.*

Right *Traditional Singaporean 'shop-houses' are tall, deep and narrow terraced buildings consisting of a series of dark rooms alternating with lightwells. This example was transformed by architect Chan Soo Khian, who opened up the building to allow daylight to drench the space. This interior now has a distinctly Japanese feel, with a wooden screen partially obscuring the view beyond. Keeping the interior open increases the circulation of cool air. Sleekly defined dark-tiled water pools offer the added bonus of cooling the air as it flows through the building.*

Air is omnipresent and vital; when clean and pure it is life-enriching, when polluted it is destructive and choking. At times still, or in violent motion, suffused with light or pitch black, filled with sound or not quite silent, air is an unpredictable element.

Early man feared the powers associated with air – the wind, rain, thunder and lightening – and devised rites to protect himself. These beliefs still play a part in Asian life today. In Bali, cleansing rituals are performed to protect a new house from ominous spirits. In Chinese culture, where deities that inhabit the air figure prominently, home life revolves around a shrine where daily offerings are made. Traditional Thai houses were built with the main entrance facing south as it was said that ghosts came from the west. The basis of this superstition lies in climatic practicalities: breezes from the south keep the house comfortable in the hot season, while in winter, it is sheltered from north winds.

While the weather is synonymous with air, so are light and space. They are the blank canvas which forms the basis of any successful interior. The interpretation of light and space in traditional Asian building styles and modern Asian living can provide valuable ideas for international interior decoration.

It can be limiting to think of space literally as emptiness. A room that is satisfying to look at, and relaxing to be in, reflects a considered balance between positive and negative space. In Japanese Noh drama, a drumbeat followed by silence is distinctive and unique; the sound and the silence are opposite but equal. To the Japanese, the silence is not just an empty space; it is the space that gives shape to the whole. Likewise, Ikebana, the Japanese art of flower arranging, is similar in that the controlled use of a limited range of materials focuses equal attention on the arrangement and the space in which it is contained. Noh drama and Ikebana are, at once, dynamic and still.

Many Japanese architects, including Tadao Ando, take inspiration from their own culture. Ando says, 'Instead of simply pursuing superficial comforts, I re-examine what has been discarded in the process of economic growth and seek after only those things that are essential to human dwelling.' In a traditional Japanese room, tatami flooring, paper *shoji* screens and sliding panels, and earth-toned mud and wood walls unify the interior through the use of natural materials. This sense of calm and order can be achieved in a less austere environment when natural materials are included, furniture carefully chosen, and a few precious objects given space and focus. With thought and restraint, it is entirely possible to create interiors that are ordered, sensual and relaxing, even if they happen to be small.

Above *The central atrium of this modernized Singaporean shop-house has a translucent ceiling made from wooden slatted screens. Daylight pouring through the lightwell above the screens casts an ever-changing pattern of shadows on the neutrally toned walls, the stone and wood floor and the water pools below. A strategically placed sculpture takes full advantage of the framing effect of the natural light. Designed for a Japanese art dealer, the decoration and furnishings are distinctly minimalist in style, yet they are successfully housed in a traditional building.*

Asian cities are as crowded, polluted and inhospitable as their Western counterparts, if not more so, as rampant modernization has destroyed much of what was architecturally unique to each country. But today there is a backlash against a glut of badly conceived architecture. A growing number of respected architects, including Geoffrey Bawa in Sri Lanka, William Lim and Kerry Hill in Singapore and Charles Correa in India, are re-examining traditional building methods and local vernacular styles to influence new construction. William Lim explains, 'Tradition and modernity are like yin and yang — they should complement each other.' The result is a renaissance of an Asian architecture that works within its surroundings.

A tangible connection with Nature is a defining aspect of Asian living, with the division of inside and outside space less clear than in the West. One of the joys of the tropical climate is being able to live in houses that do not need glass to keep out cold weather. In South-east Asia, decks, gardens, pools and walkways connect inside and outside spaces. Frequently they consist of a series of open terrace pavilions, one for entertaining, another for worship, and others for private family use. In southern India and Sri Lanka, houses built around a central courtyard allow air to circulate between the internal spaces.

Overhanging eaves, foliage, trellises, screens and blinds shade these inside/outside areas. In China, traditional family compounds are also built around a central courtyard, which during the summer serves as a meeting place, outdoor eating room and flexible extension of the private rooms around it. In the winter this space becomes a focus for contemplation.

Another aspect of traditional Asian dwellings is the division between public space, where visitors are entertained, and private family space. Open pavilions, *salas* in Thailand, *bales* in Bali or *pendopos* in Java, are transitional areas between the exterior world and the private living areas. In colonial houses, which took their inspiration from the local vernacular, verandahs served the same function, where guests were entertained in a cool environment. In Japan the entrance hall, *genkan* (entrance hall), is the transitional space, where outdoor shoes are left behind. One then steps onto a wooden platform, sometimes through a *noren* (curtain), into the private space where slippers are worn. Even the tiniest modern apartment in Japan has a *genkan* and raised floor level.

Screens are a similar device and are used inside entrances in Malaysian shop-houses to prevent a direct view into the interior. Front doors are often left open to allow breezes to flow through the house, so the screen creates privacy.

The influential Indian architect Louis Kahn said, 'I don't like to see a space nailed down. If you could move it and change it every day, fine.' This sentiment reflects an instinctive attitude to space across Asia. Multi-purpose space is a fairly new concept in interior planning in the West, whereas in Asia it is an intrinsic part of life. Cooking and bathing areas are necessarily fixed, while living and sleeping space is more flexible, allowing a room to change throughout the day. This is possible because furniture is minimal, very often limited to a raised platform or bed. In the sparsely furnished rooms of Japan, the use of tatami mats allowed the floor to become the seating, eating and sleeping area, while in Indonesian long-houses rattan matting sufficed. The Japanese futon mattress, stored in a cupboard during the day, thus freeing up the living space, must be the epitome of flexible, minimal living.

'Light is by far the most important element, without it there is no visible perception of space', states Douglas Young, a Hong Kong architect. Contrasted light and shade create complexity and depth, defining space and form, and bringing texture and variation to interior space. As Louis Kahn said, 'No space, architecturally, is space unless it has natural light.'

Tropical houses have dark interior spaces, as light brings unwanted heat. The teak houses of northern Thailand have shuttered windows allowing minimal daylight to filter inside. In Japan, sliding translucent screens admit diffused light. The ambience created by the controlled use of natural light is peaceful and meditative, while badly devised artificial light will kill the atmosphere in any room. Sensitive lighting creates an atmosphere that is calm and evocative.

Above *Asian interiors tend to be dark, shadowy spaces, providing respite from the intensity of the tropical heat and light. In contrast, this family home designed by Kerry Hill Associates in Singapore, the light is diffused through modern aluminium blinds. One side of this corridor is flanked by an outdoor pool, which has a cooling effect on the air entering through glazed doors. The interior is monochromatic with few personal possessions on display. A large paper lantern by American-Japanese sculptor Isamu Noguchi offers a semi-opaque silhouette against the luminosity of the window.*

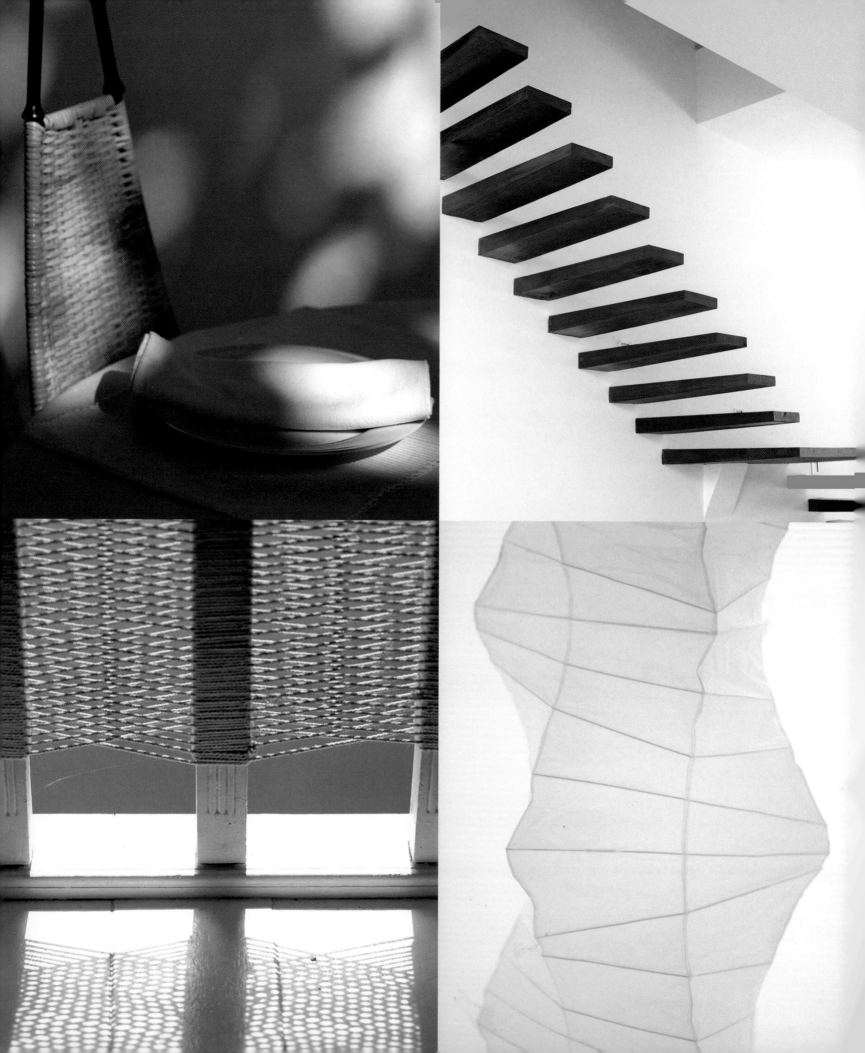

Previous spread *Light defines space and changes its feel throughout the day. Translucent materials such as fine cotton and muslin, paper, woven cane and rope provide textural contrasts with solid stone walls, wood furniture and stairways.*

From left to right *1 The texture of a woven cane dining chair is echoed by the patterns of dappled light. 2 Tapered solid wood stairs appear to float in a light-filled interior. 3 The fluid, diaphanous qualities of a muslin mosquito net are counterpointed by a rectilinear black towel rail and wrought-iron four-poster bedframe. 4 A 200-year-old Japanese lamp uses a combination of fragile white paper and solid black wrought iron. 5 An ordinary handrail decorated with lengths of string, woven through the balusters to create geometric patterns on the whitewashed wooden floor. 6 A section of a translucent Isamu Noguchi paper lantern which hints at the influence of French sculptor Brancusi. 7 Lengths of fine cotton are draped over a curtain rail to filter the sunlight streaming into this Indonesian house. 8 Doors and shutters are flung open in a Singapore shophouse. The curiously shaped window above the door is known as a 'bat light'.*

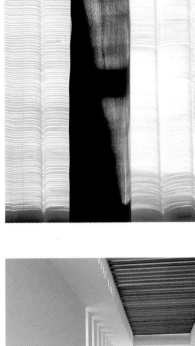

Left Asian interiors often maintain a strong link with the natural world. In this contemporary Singaporean home designed by Ernesto Bedmar, a South American living in Asia, a wide turn in the entrance corridor houses a rare reclining Chinese chair with a retractable footstool. Elements of both Asian and South American cultures can be detected in the Moorish flavour of the wall and ceiling screens, which allow a veiled view of the gardens.

Right above Light diffused through muslin falls on a polished antique teakwood plinth, silhouetting the primitive pot displayed on it. During the day, sunlight and heat are kept at bay by simple bamboo blinds and inexpensive finely woven cotton curtains, allowing air to percolate through the unglazed windows and casting atmospheric shadows across the interior.

Right below The corridor leading to the corner shown opposite serves as a cool and airy entrance hall. The simple ceiling screen of parallel wooden beams and the chunky latticework door slant the direction of the light throughout the day. With this ever-changing play of light and shade, the corridor is a pleasant, cooling haven.

Thompson silk to diffuse both the light and the heat. When one layer proved insufficient, a second was added, this time in a complementary shade of golden green, creating a triple-layer effect that both frames and screens the view to the outside world. The understated interior combines simple shapes and natural linens to create a comfortable, relaxing space. The low-level tables, Chinese in feel, and Japanese-style lamps, add to the equivocal 'Asian effect' which is a hallmark of all Liaigre's work.

Left Translucent paper shoji screens at the window filter muted daylight into this corner of a traditional Japanese tatami room. This alcove, or tokonoma, a feature of all tatami rooms, is used to display a select group of symbolic objects — usually a hanging scroll (kakemono) and a piece of pottery or floral arrangement (ikebana). The display changes with the seasons, and this softly lit space serves as a place for contemplation and a focus for meditation.

Right The sombreness of many traditional Asian interiors has here been adapted to a modern design. The Thai-inspired hardwood screen doors separate a formal Thai room from a contemporary dining room in this Bangkok house. Decoration is minimal, with strong colour counterpointed by light and dark wood forming the major statement. The tones of the unlined silk curtains are echoed in the three lampshades in graduating tones of amber above the dining table. Harsh sunlight diffused through layers of filmy fabric creates a sensual, glowing atmosphere, combining serenity with understated luxury.

Previous spread This 'glass cube' living space was designed by American architect Frank Williams, for a Thai/Japanese couple living in Bangkok. While the monumental scale of the floor-to-ceiling glass windows provides a direct link with the lush gardens beyond, it also tends to intensify the searing city heat. French designer Christian Liaigre has used layers of unlined Jim

Above *Viewed through the gauze of a fine cotton mosquito net, the rooms of this Sri Lankan hotel are flooded with light from windows on all sides. Every surface is painted white, harmonizing the space and setting off the choice of furniture and objects on display. The furniture is Dutch colonial hardwood, with natural tones carried through in the coir matting and the earthy hues of the striped cotton upholstery fabrics.*

Left *This Japanese dining room combines traditional building techniques with a resolutely contemporary aesthetic, dominated by the shoji screens which diffuse light, accentuating the mellow, understated atmosphere. Their graph-like lines are carried through into the rest of the room, broken only by the curves of a circular wooden bowl. Rectangles of karakami (literally 'paper of China') line the wall to shoulder height, preventing the fibres of the mud wall from rubbing onto clothes. The warm, earthy tones of the wall and paper are complemented by the indigo blues of the Chinese sitting carpet, highlighted by the softly filtered light.*

Above *Natural light floods unimpeded into this spacious dining room in Sri Lanka, constantly changing the atmosphere of the room. A series of simple bamboo blinds, set discreetly between each of the pillars, can be pulled down if desired, but otherwise the living space merges almost imperceptibly with the natural world around it, the setting providing a magnificent view of the water beyond.*

Previous spread *Space is a luxury in all cities, but Asian cities boast some of the most expensive real estate in the world. In order to unify and optimize the space available in this Hong Kong apartment, the owner/architect Mike Tonkin made the bold decision to use just one colour, white (not generally a popular colour in Chinese culture as it is associated with death). Built in the 1970s (and therefore old in Hong Kong terms), the apartment has a simple, compact layout. The grill-covered windows, which start at waist level, provide an urban view during the day, while at night, white light-blocking roller blinds shut out the outside world, cocooning the inhabitants in a neutral haven. Tonkin has taken the typically Asian concepts of the day-bed and futon and reinterpreted them for a contemporary environment: using cotton drill-covered foam stretching the full width of the room, the 'floor-bed' is large enough to sit six comfortably. To the right hangs a rope hammock seat, and on the floor, painted a blue-white with deck paint, stand tall white church candles and an opalescent spherical rubber posture seat. Personal possessions are stored in the bedroom and bathroom, keeping the lines of this main room uncluttered, and adding to the precious sense of space.*

Left *In this living room in Sri Lanka, the space is broken up by a simple dividing shelf system, consisting of narrow iron vertical ladders fixed permanently, top and bottom, with wooden cross shelves. The shelves are dotted with a few sculptural pieces, avoiding the dense effect of the bookcase beyond. The result is one of receding layers of vertical and horizontal lines which draw the eye to the covered verandah beyond.*

Above *This glass table — a modern take on the traditional Chinese scholar's desk and belonging to Japanese art director Kaoru Watanabe — holds calligraphy books, paintbrushes and ink blocks, beneath a 1950s' American chrome lamp. To the left, a framed 300-year-old Korean embroidery (the ends of a bolster cushion) is displayed on a Josef Hoffmann dining chair designed at the beginning of the twentieth century.*

Previous spread *The more limited the space, the more vital is the provision of storage space. Too much clutter can become overwhelming, so objects need to be chosen for their aesthetic or functional qualities.*
From left to right *1 A traditional Thai temple door-latch reinterpreted in a modern context using matt white paint. 2 A range of zitan wood Chinese scholar's brush-pots are ideal for storing desk equipment. 3 A simple hanging rail for storing clothes in a tiny bedroom. 4 Entrance curtains, or noren, such as these are a common sight throughout Japan. 5 A selection of Chinese chops (carved printing block symbols), locks and objects on display. 6 String and bulldog-clips used to display an Indonesian furniture sculptor's ideas. 7 The paraphernalia of a Chinese scholar is displayed in a large brush-pot. 8 Vellum- and leather-covered Chinese trunks make ideal storage containers.*

Right *White is again used as a unifying device in this small urban apartment, focusing attention on the objects on display and seeming to push the walls outwards visually. The parquet flooring, white walls and rigid symmetry are softened by the natural materials and organic forms. The formal arrangement of the furniture permits maximum use of the space but avoids any danger of clutter and claustrophobia. Limited colour is introduced through objects and furnishings, and in the paintings on the walls. Favouring natural materials, the owner/ designer, Debra Little, has combined the veined marble of the table with a variety of wooden objects, ceramics and cushions woven out of fine straw. The chairs are by Charles and Ray Eames. A simple bench spanning the width of the room holds Chinese artifacts.*

Far left *Simple but effective lighting solutions have been incorporated into this house on the Indonesian island of Sumbawa. High in the rush and bamboo eaves of the main living space hang lines of naked low-wattage bulbs, strung from narrow horizontal lengths of teakwood. The effect is low-key, but dramatic, rather like a simple chapel.*

Left *In the dining area of the same house hangs another cluster of bare low-wattage bulbs, this time sheathed in small woven rattan fish traps, shedding a pleasantly soft ambient light. The dining area occupies a corner of a large open-plan space in which this lighting arrangement adds focus, helping to define and separate the area from the rest of the room. The bulbs hang over a table made of highly polished insect-eaten hardwood designed by the house's owner, Jérôme Abel Séguin, and decorated with a large platter made by the Batak tribe of Sumatra. Behind hangs an enormous ceremonial tubular sarong from Sulawesi, made from pulverized tree fibre.*

Right *Paper lanterns are used in tremendous variety in northern Asia. The floor lamp here is by Isamu Noguchi, while the nineteenth-century Chinese storage cabinet from Shandong province is topped by a group of prototype lanterns designed by the owners of the apartment, artists Brad Davis and Janis Provisor. The designs are based on the forms of traditional Chinese festival lanterns, which would have been constructed in wire and fine tissue or silk, usually in very vibrant colours. These lanterns are in a heavier paper, and the traditional design has been modified and pared down to suit a contemporary environment.*

Left This small courtyard garden in Japan links the interior with the outside world in typical Asian fashion. It is viewed through a series of sliding wooden screens, creating a geometrically framed view, featuring a series of clearly defined spaces, in contrast to the more relaxed, unconscious framing seen in the Indonesian house on the right. The garden is a combination of controlled natural forms (the trees, stone and bamboo fountain) and geometry, with the simple grid pattern of the foreground screens repeated in the high wood fencing beyond.

Right above This Indonesian beach house is open to the elements along the whole of its ocean-facing side. Overhanging eaves protect the interior from the worst of the elements, while bamboo blinds serve the dual purpose of creating shade and framing the dramatic horizontal view of the ocean in the distance. Ironwood trunks support the eaves, echoing the vertical lines of the palm trees and the sculptural installation in the distance. To add to this virtually infinite sense of space and reflect light up into the interior, the owner has laid a wide path of broken white coral along the outside of the raised deck.

Right below A relaxed and informal living pavilion in Bali opens into a small ornamental garden filled with frangipani trees, with rice paddies clothing the undulating landscape beyond. Again, rolled-up bamboo blinds provide protection from wind and rain, and the Japanese owner has added sturdy sliding doors reminiscent of fusuma, the paper-covered doors seen in traditional homes in Japan.

EARTH

Previous spread *The natural world plays a fundamental part in many Asian cultures. The Balinese tropical garden is a celebration of life, filled with unrestrained colour and voluptuous forms. A seamless transition from inside to outside space characterizes this Balinese home in the hills of Ubud. Built entirely of wood and filled with sturdy Indonesian hardwood furniture, the house is set in a relaxed landscaped garden of coconut palms and bamboo, where goats and geese can wander freely.*

Right *A sealed glass window separates the display of a collection of small, early civilization terracotta pots from a large Chinese dragon water urn in this Bangkok home. Within the context of a modern air-conditioned urban environment, the inside and outside worlds have been cleverly merged through the continuity of forms and materials.*

The element Earth is the opposite of elusive Air. It possesses tangible qualities; it is tactile, sensual, imbued with colour, even smell. Earth is organic and alive, a source of nutrition for crops and plants. It is changeable – cool, rigid and hard, or warm, malleable and soft. Earth materials, such as clay and stone, become more beautiful and alive with age, made characterful by the passing of time and the onslaught of the elements.

Ancient philosophers believed the earth was a female living creature, made powerful by the male sun. In the East, feminine Earth is symbolized by the dark and curvaceous yin, the opposite of straight, male yang. The Chinese 't'sung' is a primitive object carved in jade, its square, immovable shape a symbol of the earth. Bali's brand of Hindu animism (a belief in the spirituality of Nature) defines their culture, while in Japan, Shintoism similarly venerates the forces of nature.

While there are similarities in the perception of earth in many religious contexts, the way materials derived from the earth are used by man is myriad. In this chapter we look at how natural materials are used in the home and how nature is interpreted in gardens man creates.

In Asia, the combination of cultural, personal and spiritual interpretation, and the variety of natural landscapes, resources and climatic differences have influenced the evolution of gardens. Despite these regional variations, Asian gardens share a direct relationship with the built environment, which contrasts with the Western pattern of the home as a fortress against less hospitable elements. The Asian garden is seen as an outside room, a natural extension of the interior of the home. In all traditional Asian building styles there is a merging of the inside and outside world, and it is at this interface, whether it be a verandah, a terrace or under the eaves of an internal courtyard, that daily life takes place. This connection is strengthened by the use of natural materials and earth colours. In countries where stone or brick is easily available, building styles have developed which are a synthesis of these materials, local skills, practical needs and spiritual beliefs. In contrast, modernist architects working in Asia during this century, from Le Corbusier and Charles Correa in India, to Tadao Ando in Japan, have attempted to bring out the innate beauty of materials in their purest form. The Zen principle of exclusion of superfluous things unifies the work of these architects who build in reinforced concrete — the modern stone. Economical, versatile and durable, reinforced concrete must be the defining building material of the twentieth century. While concrete does not have the immediate sensual appeal of natural stone, when in the hands of visionary architects it can be beautiful.

Above *How often do we look really closely at stone? Only by observing variations in colour, texture and pattern can we learn to appreciate its unique qualities. In Japan, Zen monks incorporate it into the designs of temple gardens: here, raked gravel and a mound of moss symbolize ocean and land in an abstract, sculptural way. Low in maintenance, high in visual impact, and ideally suited to hectic urban lifestyles, Zen-style gardens are enjoying growing popularity in the West. However, the planning and choice of elements in these deceptively simple gardens can easily take a lifetime to perfect.*

The uses of concrete throughout the home are diverse. As flooring it can be given a rough texture with stone aggregate, or it can be stained, polished and waxed, creating a sensuous, smooth surface. Cast in thin slabs for shelving, tables, even baths, concrete can be seen to have a natural quality that is both earthy and unpretentious. Concrete, like clay and stone, brings the textures and colours of nature inside the home. We feel comfortable with organic, harmonious natural colour and find it calming. The natural beauty of earth materials is most clearly drawn out when used in a straightforward, functional way, but this functionality does not preclude sensuality.

Our instinctive attraction to traditionally crafted objects is because they combine clean, practical, undecorated forms with natural materials. It is perhaps the pre-civilization pottery of Thailand's Ban Chieng period that most eloquently describes this symbiosis in clay. These simple terracotta pots were created in the latter part of the period, between 300 BC and 200 AD. Only discovered in 1966, their original use is not known, but today they are highly collectable, and fit perfectly into natural, pared down interiors. While Ban Chieng pottery is a rarefied example of Asian crafts, it is possible to collect objects and home accessories that resonate with the same qualities of nature and simplicity of form, without being prohibitively expensive. Earthenware stone and lava stone pots are versatile and inexpensive, while stone mortars come in an array of sizes.

While early man lived in harmony with the earth, we are now removed from it. It is only in the garden that man rediscovers his natural roots, satisfying a primal need to be connected with nature. When one thinks of the Asian garden, there are two extremes that come to mind. One is the Japanese dry rock and gravel garden — esoteric and inscrutable; the other is the luscious tropical garden of South-east Asia. Physically so different, yet, as celebrations of nature, they ultimately achieve the same goal.

It is arguably the island of Bali that evokes the strongest image of a tropical Asian paradise. Bali is a gardener's heaven, given such rich volcanic soil, ample rain and sunshine, everything thrives. It is an island where glistening rice terraces define the cultivated landscape, contrasting with unrestrained jungle of giant bamboo, and hardwood forest draped in giant vines, ferns and orchids. The Balinese garden is an extension of this voluptuous landscape, simulating the natural order, scale and balance of the jungle. Even humble family compounds centre around a well-tended garden. Intricately designed pathways of brick or stone lead to religious shrines. Waxy flowers, such as bubble-gum pink ginger or vermilion and lemon heliconia, and exotic fruit trees including papaya, banana, lychee, breadfruit, jackfruit and the potent smelling durian, are commonplace. The Balinese garden is a celebration of raw, unrestrained, exuberant Nature.

In contrast, from the 'strolling gardens' of Kyoto's Buddhist temples that evoke the natural order of the Japanese landscape, to the minimalist Zen gardens that use a limited range of materials, the traditional Japanese garden is an exercise in control. The Master Gardener uses the scale, proportion and balance of carefully placed plants and trees, moss, rocks and water to create an impression of distant vistas in the limited space of a formal garden. Colour is also controlled, allowing the leaf shape, scale and shades of green to provide textural interest. Often only red flowers are included, as red is the complementary colour to green. Pathways lead through bamboo groves, winding up mountainsides through carpets of moss, and past thickets of trees. The walker is given tantalizing glimpses of what lies beyond, the views deliberately obscured until a point where the vista opens up, allowing the walker to see for the first time the perfect view the gardener has planned. While the dry Zen garden is a more abstract representation of nature, using stone, gravel and sand to create islands and rippling water, all Japanese gardens can be seen as three-dimensional still-life paintings, frozen and meditative.

While most of us have no choice but to exist in an urban environment, we still have a need to feel close to nature. By surrounding ourselves with earth materials in our homes and gardens, we come a little closer to satisfying this innate desire.

Above *Concrete is the universal modern building material, with both positive and negative results. An essential factor in the rapid modernization of Asia, it allows for cheap housing, often resulting in monstrous, inhuman cities. Although frequently nondescript in appearance, it has been made into an unexpected feature in this Indonesian house. When whitewashing the room, the owner left a rectangle of grey concrete exposed: waxed and polished, flush with the rest of the wall, it now creates a defining frame around the objects on display.*

Previous spread *The variety of plants and flowers found across Asia is kaleidoscopic.*

From left to right *1 Heliconia leaves. 2 Softly fragrant frangipani flowers. 3 Lush foliage in a Balinese garden. 4 Trunks of giant green bamboo. 5 The lotus flower, an ever-present image in religious art throughout South-east Asia. 6 Ripe jack-fruit, only one of the region's many exotic fruits. 7 The waxy flowers of the peace lily (spathiphyllum). 8 A leaf from the mulberry bush (the sole diet of silkworms) in northern Thailand.*

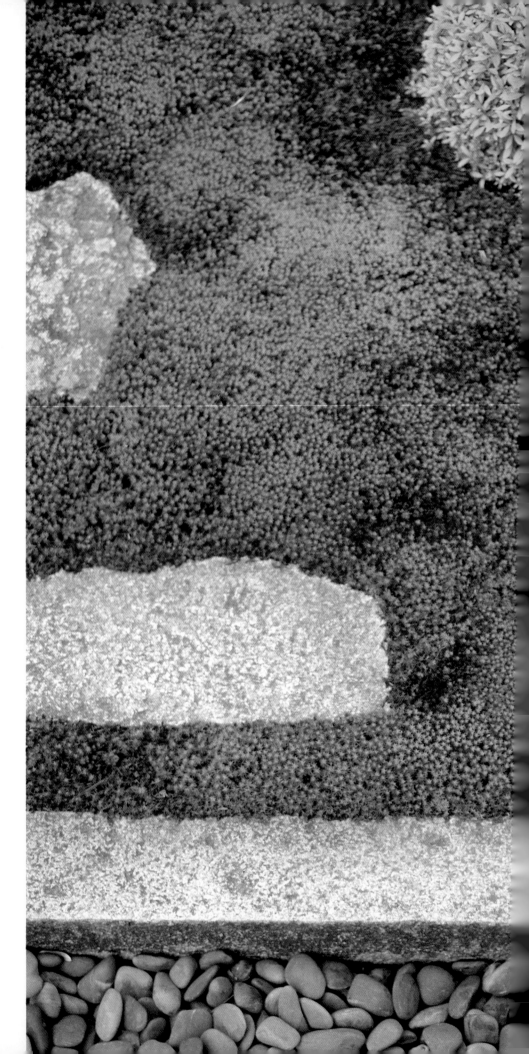

Left *This Japanese garden is an artfully simple combination of stone, gravel, moss and clipped azaleas, the vivid lime green of their leaves contrast with the stone and form a perfect complement to it.*

Right *In a Sri Lankan garden, a chequerboard pattern of hardy grass and concrete slabs makes an imaginative alternative to a plain lawn.*

Above *Concrete slabs imprinted with leaves during the drying out process are a common sight in Sri Lanka. This path leads through a dark avenue of banana, palms and heliconia, opening out unexpectedly onto a view of a coconut palm lawn and the ocean beyond.*

Above This modern interpretation of the traditional Japanese stone garden combines a 'lawn' of small, grey pebbles with a swirling pattern of slender, hand-made, matt-black ceramic tiles. Designed to be looked at rather than walked upon, it forms an eye-catching abstract composition, contrasting perfectly with the smooth stone and glass planes of the surrounding architecture.

Left Shallow steps in a Japanese garden combine slabs of rock with gravel stones in a design that is not only beautiful and unusual but also practical. Together, stones and rocks form part of a path that winds its way up a landscaped hillside, and their apparently precarious construction obliges walkers to concentrate on their feet rather than on the scene around them, postponing the view of the garden until the walker reaches the gardener's chosen vantage point.

Above *This entrance path to a modern house in Singapore by architect Ernesto Bedmar could be viewed as a reinterpretation of a Japanese rock garden. It consists of a series of large rectangular granite blocks that appear to float in a sea of stones. While loose stones and pebbles can often be uncomfortable underfoot, this stepping-stone device is easy to walk on and impressive to look at.*

Right *In this imposing entrance courtyard, also in Singapore, Ernesto Bedmar has used a combination of pebble and stone blocks once more, this time setting them in concrete. The swirling pattern evokes the pathways introduced to the region by the Portuguese colonials, while also recalling the undulating lines of sand in traditional Japanese gardens. One could imagine the solid wood door and square closure to be the entrance to a Buddhist temple.*

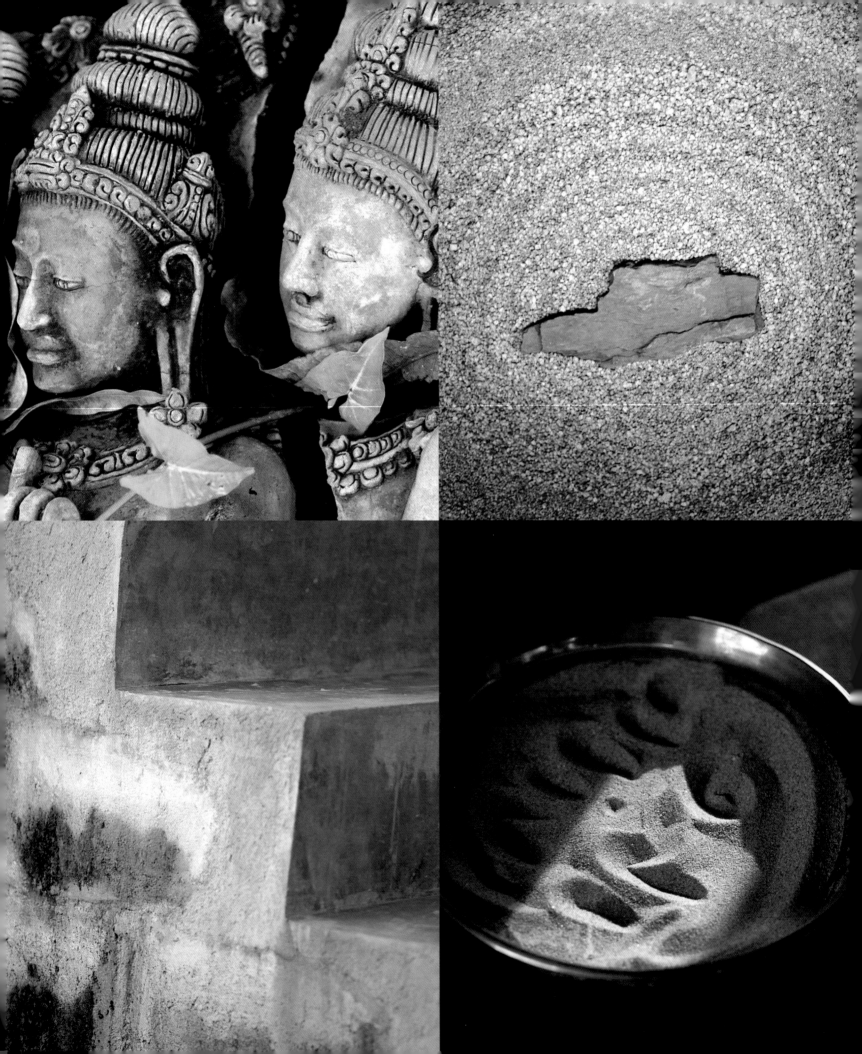

Previous spread *Smooth or rough, weather-beaten or freshly cast, cool and damp or warmed by the sun, earth materials all ask to be experienced through touch.* **From left to right** *1 Weathered terracotta heads from a Chang-Mai workshop in northern Thailand. 2 A shard of black slate encircled by precisely raked gravel. 3 Detail of a concrete slab imprinted with the image of leaves. 4 A blanket of woven jasmine flowers draped over a sea-weathered concrete Buddhist shrine. 5 Stone steps distressed and coloured by seawater, rain and heat. 6 A glistening brass dish filled with fine sand, highlighted by evening sunlight. 7 Shards of granite, pebbles and a traditional woven shawl explore the diversity and subtlety of grey and stone tones. 8 Detail of a Chinese celadon stool.*

Right *This southern Sri Lankan villa, Claughton, is the work of architect Geoffrey Bawa. Taking inspiration from tropical building styles combined with a modernist sensibility, Bawa's buildings are a fusion of the traditional and the contemporary. Transitional inside/outside spaces are one of his hallmarks; here the multi-level living area serves a number of different functions. The main space is dominated by a built-in concrete seating area. Colour is monochrome, the earth and stone tones of the paintwork and floor echoed in the low-key cotton canvas furnishings. A swirling driftwood sculpture softens the uncompromising geometry.*

Above *Architectural detail in Bawa's work is pared
down, never ornate. Here the materials tell the story.
A robust wall of rough stone creates continuity with the
exterior landscape. A refined contrast is introduced by
the wrought-iron balustrade, adding a well-defined clean
line against the jagged rock. Concrete is whitewashed
and the stairs are a rugged, sandy texture.*

Previous spread *Cool colours and hard edges take on an unexpected softness in the tropical climate of Southeast Asia. In intense sunlight, strong interior colour can become too concentrated and oppressive, while carpets and soft furnishings are cloying in the humidity and heat. Surprisingly, perhaps, concrete offers a cool, clean-lined alternative. This waxed concrete table was conceived by Geoffrey Bawa for The Villa hotel in Bentota. Determinedly monochromatic, the scene is a study in serenity. Sitting under a deep, overhanging verandah, the unusually shaped table has an uninterrupted view of a swimming pool and palm grove beyond. The chairs are arranged as the architect intended, with the outer edge of the table left exposed. Simple, high-backed wrought-iron and cane chairs lend a further element of formal/informal ambiguity, while the white-painted concrete service table to the rear is sheltered by ornately decorative woodwork, no doubt salvaged from a colonial villa.*

Left *This gallery-style space is defined by a tall staircase in wax-polished concrete. Non-existent building restrictions in this part of Indonesia mean that handrails can be dispensed with, therefore leaving the grey jagged line of the stairs clean and abstract against the whitewashed walls. The concrete was hand-mixed to attain the exact shade of grey required, slightly paler than the tone of the floor. Decorative detail is avoided in this interior and the furniture is simple and functional, allowing variations of colour and texture in the concrete and wood to keep the eye gently occupied.*

Right *This concrete staircase in a Sri Lankan house has a solid whitewashed handrail detailed with a strip of highly polished concrete. The three circular metal platters, juxtaposed with the rectilinear lines of the staircase, complement the natural textures and tones of the concrete while echoing its qualities of coolness and rigidity.*

In all primitive cultures, buildings and shelters are constructed from whatever material is most readily available. Clay (or mud) — abundant, malleable and versatile — is the universal building material. Yama-tsuchi, literally 'mountain dirt', is the name given to this highly evolved style of mud construction in Japan. A latticework of bamboo tied with wisteria vine is constructed inside a frame of wood. Between three and seven layers of yama-tsuchi (a combination of soil, clay and rice straw) are applied to a layer of hemp fibres, to help prevent shrinkage away from the wooden frame as the mud dries out. The end result of this painstaking and skilled process is an even-textured, earth-coloured surface. Derived solely from the natural dirt mixture, the precise tone is unique to each batch and therefore impossible to touch up at a later date. The ingenious windows are literally holes left uncovered during the construction process, the visible bamboo lattice, as in these circular examples, simply an extension of the internal framework.

Left *A view of Claughton, the Geoffrey Bawa-designed house which sits on a rocky headland on the southern tip of Sri Lanka, looking out across the vast emptiness of the Indian Ocean. A drought-parched lawn falls away to a steep, stony drop, plunging to the waves beneath. Coconut palms create shade, while spiky desert plants add sculptural shape. The house was constructed using local materials, combining the traditional vernacular of tropical buildings with a contemporary sensibility. The house is laid out as a series of comfortable entertaining and living areas orientated towards the spectacular ocean view. Inside/outside architecture and natural materials — stone and wood — echo the external environment, effectively merging the man-made construct with its natural environment.*

Right *In central Bali, John and Cynthia Hardy have created this extraordinary 'tree-house' with architect Yen Kuan Cheong, perched on land overlooking a river gorge. Terraced rice paddies and monsoon rainforest define the landscape in this area near Ubud. Constructed entirely of wood, the house becomes an integral part of the landscape, its bedrooms, bathrooms and formal living rooms raised on tall ironwood telegraph poles. Beneath is a series of outside living areas and an indoor/outdoor kitchen (with glass walls that can be closed to allow for air conditioning). The building rises from a relaxed garden, landscaped with pools and paths.*

WOOD

Previous spread *Wood is the enduring passion of the owner of this bedroom in Sumbawa, Indonesia. In the eaves of his barn-like house, French furniture designer, Jérôme Abel Séguin has created dramatically simple bedrooms using a few key ingredients. The roof is made from traditional alang-alang rush tied to horizontal poles of bamboo. Wood floors are left unpolished, while the mattress sits on a glossy rattan mat made in Kalimantan. A solid bench made from salvaged construction teakwood supports a simple lamp made from a slice of giant bamboo, while the tall paper lantern is by Isamu Noguchi. The loosely formed leather 'bowl' in the foreground was made on the island of Lombok.*

Right *The library of the Amanjiwo hotel in Java contains elements from throughout the Asian continent. While Indonesian in essence, it has the coolness and graphic quality of a Japanese tatami room, while the walls are hung with a display of Chinese export-ware ceramic plates. A dark chocolate-coloured heavy slub-cotton lines the walls and is used to cover the traditional quilted mattress. The room's most striking feature is the screen of pale wood surrounding the full-sized daybed.*

Wood is the living natural element. It is versatile, organic and diverse. In its natural state, wood symbolizes growth. Every inch of a length of wood is unique; its grain and depth of colour constantly changing. Wood brings the relaxing tones of nature into the home; from translucent Chinese paper to dark Indonesian ironwood. Without wood, a home would be without a soul.

In this chapter we look at how the use of wood in buildings and interiors creates continuity with the natural world. We also look at the range of materials associated with wood, including organic natural fibres for weaving and paper making.

Today all-wood buildings in Asia are increasingly rare. Availability of materials goes hand in hand with the evolution of vernacular design, and although historically wood has been readily available, depleted resources and modern materials have resulted in a more sparing use of it.

In tropical Asia peasant dwellings would have been timber structures with a woven rush or shingle roof. Palaces and merchant houses were also made, at least in part, of wood. More elaborate in style, they still incorporated similar features: wood floors, pitched roofs, overhanging eaves and verandahs. Many structures were on stilts, raising the living quarters from the mud in the wet season and allowing cool air to flow through floorboards.

Colonial architecture in Asia was also predominantly of wood construction, but as a fusion of nostalgic European styles with practical elements of the local vernacular, they often resulted in quaint houses that palpably hankered after a different continent. A combination of cheap materials like concrete and brick, the increasing rarity of hardwood, and a move towards a globally influenced architecture has seen these vernacular forms dying out. Ironically it is now usually either the very rich or the very poor that live in hardwood houses. However, there are a number of architects that have incorporated elements of traditional wood buildings into their modern Asian homes.

The use of recycled hardwoods in architectural detailing creates a sense of authenticity and appropriateness. This can be seen in flooring, in exposed structural beams or screens, in partitions and in blinds. Concern about the diminishing supply of hardwood has inspired designers to use alternative resources such as porcupine-grained coconut palm, rich yellow and plentiful jack-wood, and the miracle material — bamboo.

Fast-growing and widely available, bamboo shoots or 'culms' can be harvested within five years. Its cellular structure makes bamboo both strong and light (it has a tensile strength greater than that of steel) while its outer skin is waterproof. One of the miraculous sights in Asia today is the construction site. It is an extraordinary marriage of old and new technology, where a skyscraper will be constructed at speed by workers balancing on an outer latticework of scaffolding constructed entirely of bamboo. Bamboo can also be made into simple watertight containers and utensils; lightweight, versatile and strong furniture; durable woven panels for seating, flooring and walls; even paper.

While it is rare to live in a wood or bamboo house, many Asian homes are furnished with these natural materials. The American-born architect and furniture-maker George Nakashima discovered the beauty of wood when he went to Japan for the first time at the age of 21. He believed that if a job was carried out correctly, making a piece of furniture gave the tree a second life of dignity. Wood is such a malleable material that there is a temptation to carve and embellish it. While much Asian furniture is ornate, arguably destroying the 'spirit' of the material, there is also some exceptionally beautiful furniture which resonates with the qualities admired by Nakashima. Some of the furniture of the Chinese Ming and Qing dynasties, for example, is an exercise in understated perfection and exquisite craftsmanship, highly coveted by collectors. The classic pieces of Chinese furniture considered most desirable today include the perfectly proportioned 'altar' table; the rectilinear

Above *A combination of wood tones and textures are off-set by the cool white of the tiled floor and walls in this Balinese home. Sliding grid-like wood partitions are a traditional Japanese device and here they are crafted from honey-coloured, locally available jack-wood. In contrast, the primitive Sumatran teak bench is hewn from a single piece of wood exploiting the natural grain of the tree. A very Japanese collection of sun hats becomes a sculptural intervention, adding soft contrast to a rectilinear room and picking up the intricate weave and texture of the tribal rush floor matting.*

form of the official's hat chairs and solid, lacquered cupboards and chests. They were made from oak, elm, maple, chestnut, camphor, bamboo, and even the lacquer tree. There is now a growing number of Asian-born designers reassessing the value of their cultural heritage and interpreting these forms within a contemporary context.

While Japan adopted many things from China, including tea and paper, inexplicably it did not take chairs. China alone in Asia evolved a tradition of furniture raised off the ground, while throughout the rest of the continent people lived at floor level, on matting or low-level furniture usually constructed in wood. Functional furniture like trunks and cupboards evolved through practical necessity. Some rustic pieces from Japan and Korea are more timeless, and work well in today's aesthetic climate, as do pieces from Sumatra. Roughly hewn from teakwood, the furniture is monolithic, sometimes crude in form, but resonating with the combined lives of the tree and the craftsman who made it.

As a compromise between primitive and formally designed furniture, pieces made during the Colonial era are a fusion of Western and Chinese influences. The planter's chair is emblematic of the style – a comfortable and informal piece of furniture, it is oversized, usually teak, with bamboo cane replacing upholstery and allowing air to circulate. This combination of comfort, ease of use and practicality that translates perfectly to today.

Paper is wood, transformed from solid and opaque to fine and translucent. Discovering how to make paper ranks among the greatest of man's early achievements. Throughout Asia, a huge variety of tree and plant fibres are woven, felted or plaited, each area having its own tradition, identified by the plants used, weave patterns, method of construction and the finished product. In Sulawesi, plant fibre is pulverized and made into a tough papery felt-like fabric. From this rough, rigid fabric they make crude, but durable clothing. In Japan, rice straw is used to make plaited circular floor cushions, footwear, baskets, even wall construction and stuffing for futons. Abaca is a semi-rigid fabric made in the Philippines from coconut fibre, perfect for table mats. Across Indonesia textured plant fibres are woven into an array of products. Cedar roots become scented window blinds and bathroom mats, while hyacinth root, pandanus, mendong, lontar reeds and familiar rattan and bamboo are transformed into boxes, fabrics and flooring.

Woven natural textiles like hemp, cotton and silk contribute an element of textural contrast and colour to Asian homes. Textiles add softer areas of focus and comfort to a room, especially if natural colours are used that complement the tones and textures of wood. Each region has its own unique traditions, from the fine cotton batiks of Java, the Kasuri (Ikat) indigo cottons and Shibori (dye resist) of Japan to the luminous silks of northern Thailand and the intricate embroidery of Lombok.

From furniture to buildings, paper to textiles, it is the living aspect of wood that appeals to us in today's hard world. We need the warm, comforting and sensual element that wood brings into our homes.

Above *Light gives startling definition to this open staircase in Kyoto, Japan. In this interior composed entirely of wood, with the exception of the rough granite floor, variety is introduced through the contrasting textures and colours of the wood, and the combination of graphic and organic lines. The sliding doors, or fusuma, to the left, are covered in alternating layers of karakami, literally 'paper from China', in earthy tones. The walls are constructed from a combination of mud, hemp and rice fibre, adding a further natural element to this distinctively Japanese design.*

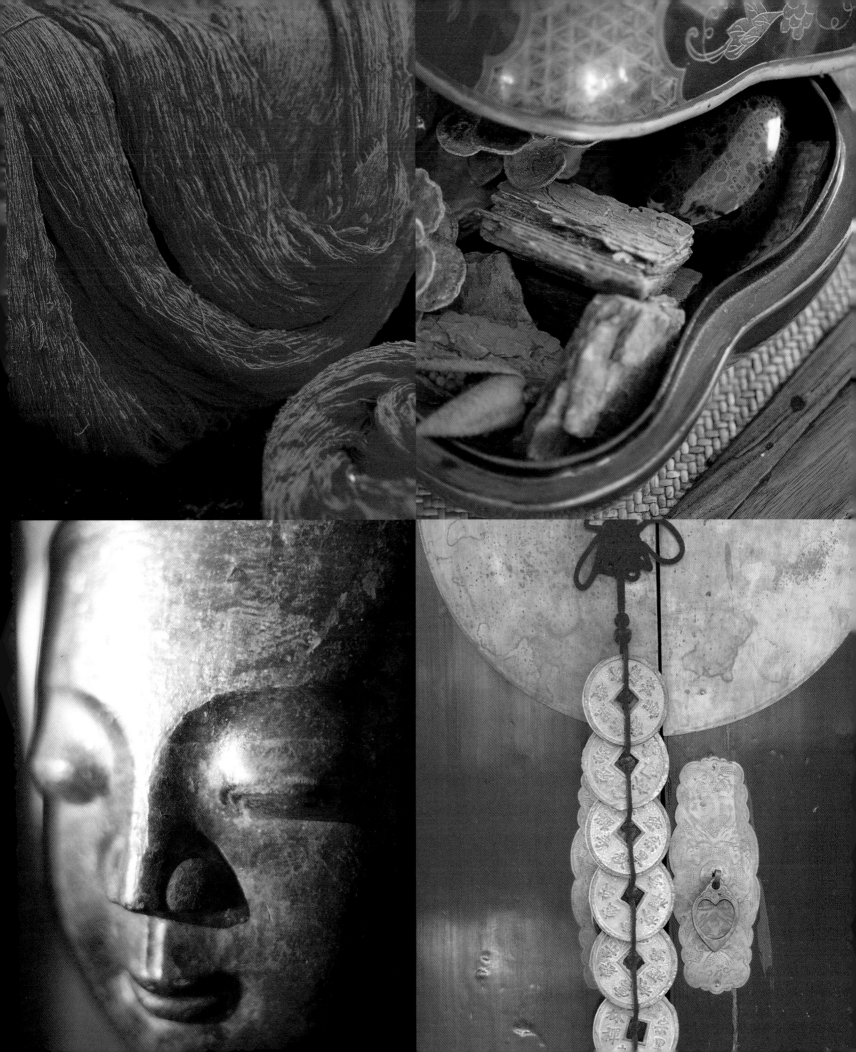

Previous spread *Wood, lacquer and gilt add richness and lustre to Asian interiors.*

From left to right *1 In this detail of a hand-painted poster, the dramatic combination of gold and red evokes the traditional festivities and celebrations of the Chinese culture. 2 The classic modernist lines of this Thai chair are softened by the addition of hollow bamboo armrests. 3 Shanks of cotton just out of the dyeing vat glow brilliant vermilion. 4 The art of display is all about unexpected and original combinations. In this Hong Kong interior, the contrasting textures of a red lacquer box and a collection of driftwood are displayed on a Chinese bench made of rattan and wood. 5 Woven patterns using natural fibres enable an infinite range of variations. 6 'Snake-fruit' is an intriguing South-east Asian fruit, which looks more inviting than it tastes: far better to display its dramatic skin in a highly polished bowl carved from coconut wood. 7 The calm and serene features of a gilded and carved wooden Buddha in Thailand. 8 Copper coins hung on a length of red thread are a familiar Chinese good luck symbol, seen here against the red lacquer and metal door furnishings of a traditional wedding cabinet.*

Left *Feng Shui dictates that books should not be displayed as the aggressive lines take away positive energy. In his Hong Kong home, Chinese architect and retail entrepreneur Douglas Young cheerfully ignores this belief, displaying his calligraphy books as part of the decorative scheme. His home is a blend of natural textures and materials (notably wood), Chinese furniture and the occasional chrome and leather Philippe Starck chair. Here, books rest on a George Nakashima wooden console against a backdrop of linen curtains. They support, among other things, a fossilized fungus and a fragment of Chinese blue and white ceramic.*

Above *The subtle natural palette used throughout the apartment is complemented by the occasional use of strong colour, here in the blue tones of the cushions and carpet, and in the glaze on a Japanese ashtray set on a nest of early twentieth-century veneered tables.*

Right *Beyond a George Nakashima bench, open shelves display a collection of creamy white ceramics and Celadon – old and new, Asian and Western – unified by a simplicity and perfection of line.*

Opposite *These elegant curved structures made of thin strips of bamboo may be seen leaning against the outside walls of houses in Japan. They originally served a somewhat esoteric purpose. Called* inu bashari, *or 'dog running', they were arranged along the external walls of merchant houses in the no-man's land between private and public space, defining a change of use. They also serve the practical purpose of preventing dogs from doing what they do naturally against walls.*

Left above *Bamboo is a familiar sight across Asia, used for everything from household utensils to major building construction. Here sections of giant bamboo cover a water drain in a Kyoto garden.*

Left centre *Fine bamboo is very malleable when young, and can be woven into intricate, layered sections to be used as exterior partitions and screens.*

Left below *Bamboo fence-making is a skilled art in Japan. This example in a private Kyoto garden makes a striking backdrop for a row of lush green acers.*

Right *Bamboo products in Indonesia are more rustic than their Japanese counterparts, but they are just as diverse and imaginative. In this Javanese house a planters' chair in recycled teak is upholstered in bamboo, while the cushion is made from the woven roots of water hyacinth. The open* sala *or* pendopo *building has bamboo blinds made by opening sections of giant bamboo, flattening them into strips, and then threading them together; the same technique was used for the mats on Chinese opium beds to provide a cooling surface.*

Right *This all-wood interior owes its dramatic impact to the combination of natural light, the generous scale and the unifying use of white. Where floorboards, wall and roof surfaces are rough, and cupboards and shelving are made of inexpensive wood, there is no point in even attempting to bring out the natural grain, colour or beauty of the wood: instead it becomes a simple and versatile building material, as is the case in this master bedroom at Sun House, Sri Lanka, a colonial house that is now an exclusive hotel, overlooking the harbour town of Galle. Built into the eaves, the room is flooded with light and warm breezes, which flow through the open windows and doors on all four sides. Although simply furnished with a colonial four-poster, bedside tables, free-standing towel rails and built-in storage, it exudes a palpable air of old-world glamour and luxury.*

Opposite *Jérôme Abel Seguin's passion for wood is unmistakable throughout his Sumbawa home and workshop. In the main bedroom, an awesome display of twisting lianne wood has been installed behind a low-level bed. Side tables are made from old grain mortars while a wooden platter is filled with flowers.*

Above *The soft tones of wood, rush and bamboo create a soothing atmosphere in this bedroom. Crisp white cotton shirts are hooked casually onto the bamboo struts of the rush roof, contributing to the purity of the colour scheme. In the foreground stands a primitive teak bird sculpture from Borneo.*

Above right *A rainforest vine, lianne wood is soft and flexible when young, hardening with age.*

Right *Colonial planters' chairs and Jérôme's monolithic furniture mingle beneath the low eaves of alang-alang, while bamboo blinds filter some of the searing heat and light. The roof is supported by pillars made from trunks of ironwood: the durability of this exceptionally dense wood, as unyielding as metal (as its name suggests), makes it impossible to work in anything but the most rudimentary way.*

Far left One of the striking differences between Asian and Western interiors is the manner in which they are furnished: in Asia, furniture is arranged in the centre of the room with space around it, while in the West, objects appear to cling to the walls. Asian living also tends to be low-level, with people habitually crouching or kneeling, while Westerners tend to sit upright on rigid chairs. This difference is especially marked in Japan, where seating is on square floor cushions called zabuton. Men sit cross-legged, while women must kneel demurely or perch with their legs swept parallel to one side — neither position found comfortable by Westerners for more than a few minutes. This large tatami room is dominated by a low-level black lacquer table, made about twenty years ago in Wajima, the centre of Japanese lacquer crafts. Its mirror-like surface reflects a tranquil garden of rocks, trees and perfectly clipped azalea bushes. The lacquered wood and paper standing lamps probably date from the early twentieth century, as does the Japanese carpet. Sliding paper shoji screens and bamboo blinds gently frame the view of the garden.

Left This house in Bali betrays the distinctive touch of its Japanese owner, most notably in the sliding wood screens, which work well in the building's clearly defined timber construction. Plain white walls form a good backdrop to an unusual collection of huge primitive Javanese furniture, and white-tiled floors continue this note of austerity.

Previous spread *Sensual and varied, wood may be as fragile as tissue paper, or as unyielding as iron: whatever its qualities, its uses are multiple.*

From left to right *1 Lengths of giant bamboo drying in the Bali sun. 2 The trunk of a coconut palm forms the support for this wooden staircase in Thailand, its warm colour off-set by the grey concrete wall. 3 Calligraphy on a Chinese paper scroll. 4 Objects displayed on a dark wood tray include this Chinese bone brush, a primitive comb and a Chinese wooden spectacle case. 5 Japanese wooden slippers, or geta, on a stone floor. 6 A cluster of Chinese calligraphy and painted scrolls. 7 Rugged three-dimensional tree bark. 8 Wood at its most delicate: slender supple stems studded with downy buds.*

Above *All rough-hewn, ethnic connotations are swept aside in this elegant Bangkok interior. The dramatic focus of the bedroom is the austere, dark-stained teakwood four-poster bed, made to the specifications of the owner, Lindsey Bailey, in a Bangkok workshop. The window behind is screened with cane blinds, stained chocolate brown and edged with cotton drill, filtering natural light and silhouetting the white bed linen. The dark wood theme is continued in the unadorned mirror to the right, and the turned-wood vessels on the side table to the left. Contrast is provided by a cane table, a woven rush cushion set on a white linen armchair, and a colonial-style Burmese table.*

Right *In this monochromatic composition by French designer Christian Liaigre, scale in a cavernous space is defined by a wall panel in wenge wood, set behind a full-size lacquered grand piano. The horizontal lines are continued by his trademark elongated sofa in neutral linens; the low table and paper lantern are Japanese in feel. The limed oak flooring strikes a warmer note. In this interior, the use of wood and natural tones — part of the essence of Japanese design — evokes an atmosphere of eastern harmony and Zen coolness.*

Opposite *Lacquering is the lengthy process of applying layers of varnish to a surface, usually wood. True lacquer is made from the sap of the sumac tree native to South-east Asia. In this modern house in Tokyo, a 'Tamba-ware' Hyan period pot, over 1000 years old, stands on a black lacquered table. Behind is a black lacquer screen designed by the owner, art director, Kaoru Watanabe. The contemporary lines of the lacquer are complemented by Le Corbusier furniture and offset by a priceless collection of Asian artifacts, including a 500-year-old red lacquer monk's rice bowl and a tenth-century* 'Sanage-ware' *dish on the wooden consul. The Edo period men's kimono bags in the foreground, some 300 years old, are made from indigo-dyed deer-skin attached to a basket of woven whale's whiskers!*

Above *Varied wood textures and colours combine to create a harmonious composition in this Bangkok home. Dark-stained teakwood contrasts with the pale rattan Indonesian mats, while a Chinese black lacquer cabinet (sporting a display of giant candles) makes an elegantly sombre background for a velvet-covered chaise-longue.*

Above In most Asian homes sleeping areas are versatile spaces, often used during the day by the whole family for napping, eating or chatting. Mattresses, thinner than their western counterparts, are easily rolled up for storage. This bedroom in the Muang Kulay Pan hotel in Koh Samui, Thailand, takes ideas from the traditional Asian bedroom and uses them in a modern context. It has a built-in raised plinth area, an idea that works well where ceilings are low, keeping the focus of the room at a low level and creating a sense of space above. The Western-style mattress is placed on a wooden plinth that frames it. The owners have used locally available coconut wood and bamboo throughout the hotel.

Right This plinth bed is made from cheap construction wood, powder-coated with a thick, lacquer-like layer of matt white paint, set on an unvarnished hardwood floor. The owner, architect Jutti Supabhundit, has inserted a tatami base into the centre, allowing air to circulate beneath the mattress – important in a humid climate. Combining European design with a rediscovered interest in Asian arts and crafts Supabhundit's apartment is filled with Western twentieth-century pieces alongside traditional Asian crafts. The collection of terracotta pots dates from the Ban Chieng period, while the lamp in front of the vertical aluminium blinds was designed by Eileen Gray in the 1920s.

FIRE

Previous spread *This modern, white kitchen is in Hong Kong, where, like the rest of Asia, it is unusual to see large kitchens designed for the whole family. The traditional Asian kitchen is often just a hot, cramped, functional cooking area, bereft of artifice. The Chinese family that lives in this cool, white space wanted a Western style kitchen that worked in an Asian home. In fact there are two kitchens, this is the family kitchen where glassware is displayed. Concealed behind is the 'working kitchen' where the messy cooking goes on.*

Right *The tea ceremony is central to Japanese culture. This four-and-a-half tatami mat tea room has a slightly unconventional layout: the open hearth, or irori, with the kettle hanging from a hook known as a jizai-kagi, would usually be in the centre of the room with the four tatami mats spiralling around it, but here it is set to one side. In this strikingly simple room, the natural light is intentionally subdued, making a wall covered with haku (gold-foil paper) glow warmly. Above and below, the haku is painted with a layer of transparent lacquer, which defines the gold and evokes the luminous quality of the American painter Mark Rothko's works.*

Fire is the illusive, powerful element. Both terrifying and inspirational, fire is at the heart of civilization. Its powers of transformation provide the means to change sand to glass and ceramic, ore to metal; to turn cold, inhospitable environments to warm, inviting ones, and enable us to transform food.

Fire is also a destructive and uncontrollable force. In Japan where houses were traditionally built of wood, the god Kagu Zuchi protects the home from the dangers of fire caused by earthquakes and high winds. In the cooler countries of North Asia, where fire is needed for heating as well as cooking during winter, domestic gods watch over the family's interests. In Japan the hearth gods are Oki-Tsu-Hiko and Oki-Tsu-Hime, while the venerated Kamado-no-Kami is god of the kitchen range. The Buddhist and Shinto gods in Japanese culture are symbolically offered the first food at meal times. The Chinese hearth god, or kitchen god, is Tsao-wang, for whom three joss sticks are lit every day.

On the following pages we look at the Asian kitchen and how it differs from kitchens in the west, as well as attitudes and rituals associated with food and eating. We also look at the Asian table, and objects made of metal and ceramic.

The fluid planning of the Asian house means that domestic activities take place in the area set between the interior and the exterior of the home. The Asian kitchen tends to be a small, functional space, often an adjunct to the home rather than the centre of it, and as in all cultures, it is traditionally the women's domain, a communal space for working and talking.

Tropical kitchens are frequently open to the elements and simply equipped with a stove, preparation table, water tap and a series of large containers in which to wash food and equipment. The basis of almost all Asian meals is rice, except in those regions where it is not possible to grow it, in which the consumption of noodles and breads has evolved instead. Rice is so much a part of everyday life that in some cultures, including Cantonese and Thai, an invitation to eat a meal translates literally as to 'eat rice'.

Entertaining at home is not fashionable in Asia in the way that it is in the West. Families often eat outside the home, and guests are frequently entertained in restaurants. Eating out is not 'an event', but an everyday occurrence, a comparatively inexpensive and informal affair. This attitude towards eating is a defining aspect of Asian life.

Twentieth-century Western lifestyles have had an impact on all areas of traditional Asian home life, not least in the kitchen. The growing appreciation of Western cooking is now evident in modern homes. The Asian kitchen today is ostensibly a Western kitchen, with the addition of specialized equipment that places it in an Eastern context. These

Above *Wherever you travel in Asia, you discover that food and eating are a way of life for most people, a preoccupation, sometimes even an obsession. In tropical Asia it is the availability of delicious and, to the Western palate, unusual fresh produce that makes eating such an enormous pleasure. Rice is still the mainstay of most Asian diets, even at breakfast-time, though foreigners may prefer a platter of tropical fruit. In Sri Lanka, a mixture of papaya, mango, watermelon and pineapple is served accompanied by a clay dish of thick, creamy buffalo curd.*

include a few electrical machines designed specifically for the Asian market – the ubiquitous rice cooker and the slow cooker for hot-pot style dishes. The main prerequisite is the gas cooker, as it provides the intense heat for wok cooking. But fire is still the focus of traditional family life in Japan during winter, when the hearth or *iori* is kept burning at all times.

Food is often imbued with ritual and ceremony in Asia. In Bali the whole community prepares the feasts for temple festivals and Chinese cultures have a tradition of special dishes for festivals and celebrations. Kaiseki cuisine is another example of how Japanese culture stylizes, transforms and elevates the everyday and mundane. Based on the traditions of the Tang dynasty, this cuisine allows the perfection of simple ingredients to be fully appreciated. The relationship between the food and the way it is displayed is paramount, with each dish constructed like a painting. So exacting is this aesthetic that a dish called *oribe- fu*, a wheat gluten dumpling, is only served in oribe pottery. Five methods of preparation are used (raw, steamed, grilled, simmered and fried); and five colours (red, blue, green, yellow, black), and five tastes (sweet, sour, hot, bitter, salty). A meal that reflects the season and the theme of a particular festival contains a balance of such elements, displayed on ceramics and lacquerware that work in harmony.

Blue and white ceramic is a popular glaze combination in China, Japan and Thailand. In Thailand the creamy eau-de-Nil shades of celadon pottery (a craft which died out in the early seventeenth century but was rediscovered around 1900) provide a neutral backdrop for the colourful, fragrant, spicy dishes. Celadon combined with local bronze cutlery creates a distinctively Thai table-top. The apparently opposite approach is taken in Japan where a contrasting but harmonious melange of textures, colours and shapes combine to make distinctive table settings. Chopsticks are used in countries where China has had an impact on the culture. Ivory, wood or bamboo chopsticks have the advantage of not overpowering flavours with metallic taste; the same is true of Chinese ceramic spoons.

China has had a huge impact on art and design worldwide. Pottery has been traded with Java and Sumatra since the tenth century, while Japan and Korea evolved their own ceramic traditions based on the influence of early Chinese dynasties. Japanese pottery is an instinctive response to clay, form and glaze, sometimes seeming ugly and discordant to the uninitiated eye. Contrastingly, pieces created during the Song dynasty (960 – 1279) are often considered the high point of Chinese ceramics. Defined by elegant forms, fine glazes and sophisticated colour – ivory, pale green, duck egg and sky blues – Song ceramics have a timeless quality, in tune with both Eastern and Western modern trends. These ceramics are now highly collectable.

The Tang dynasty (618 – 907) is considered the golden age of the Chinese Empire. The arts created during this period were influenced by Buddhism and by the trade routes that brought ideas from Rome, Athens and Iran. The distinctive three colour glazes of Tang pottery, iron for red, yellow and brown tones, copper oxide for greens, and cobalt for blue, were inspired by imported coloured silks. What unifies these two different ceramic traditions is their pleasing shape and the choice of glaze, which highlights the perfection of form.

Bronze casting is another art form that appeals to our contemporary tastes for primal forms and simple decorative motifs. The design of twelfth century Shang dynasty bronze vessels and pots were based on everyday objects, but because bronze was a valuable material, they were only used for special rituals. Bronze ornaments found in Northern Thailand from the Ban Chieng period are also imbued with this beauty and simplicity. But it is arguably the image of Buddha, often cast in bronze and covered in a layer of gold, seen throughout Asia, that most eloquently evokes visual serenity and perfection.

It is to this idea of perfection and beauty in simple things and mundane tasks associated with Asian culture that we are drawn to today. There is still much we can learn from traditional Asian attitudes towards food and the rituals associated with eating. Eating should not be a daily necessity but a unique celebration.

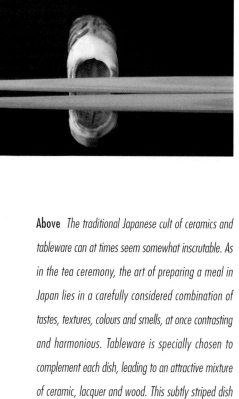

Above *The traditional Japanese cult of ceramics and tableware can at times seem somewhat inscrutable. As in the tea ceremony, the art of preparing a meal in Japan lies in a carefully considered combination of tastes, textures, colours and smells, at once contrasting and harmonious. Tableware is specially chosen to complement each dish, leading to an attractive mixture of ceramic, lacquer and wood. This subtly striped dish is by master potter Rosanjin Kitaoji, (1883–1959), while the delicate blue and white chopstick rest comes from China.*

Previous spread *Delicious food in Asia ranges from the simple to the sublime: from a delectable bowl of curry and rice from a Bangkok street hawker to an exquisitely prepared Japanese feast.*

From left to right *1 Rice-flour cakes shaped to look like apples and flat Shanghai biscuits sweetened with honey are traditionally served at all Chinese celebrations. 2 Wooden skewers of Indonesian chicken saté served with a bowl of spicy peanut sauce. 3 Chillies, lime juice, shallots, garlic and fish sauce make a perfect accompaniment to deep-fried minced pork balls in Thailand. 4 The haute cuisine of sushi – a careful arrangement of abalone, kohada (fillets of small, silvery fish), torigai (a squid-like shellfish) and bonito. 5 A selection of sticky rice and bean sweets from Thailand, made in individual banana-leaf cups. 6 Pumpkin with a coconut milk and egg-custard filling, sweetened with palm sugar and flavoured with pandanus leaf, sliced and served on a banana leaf. 7 Fast-food Indonesian style: a neat package of rice, meat curry and vegetables wrapped in a cone of brown paper. 8 A soup of snapper, spring onions, celery leaves, lemon grass, garlic and shallots coloured vibrant yellow with turmeric.*

Left *Plywood fittings add warmth to the concrete and stainless steel of this contemporary kitchen.*

Above *Metal sieves with bamboo handles are used for draining noodles and rescuing food from the wok.*

Right *On a high-tech stove a wok rests on a solid rim.*

Below *Wooden spoons contrast with a darker wood bowl, with a paler bamboo whisk in the background.*

Left Even where space is limited, a dining table creates a social area, a place for communication and shared enjoyment of food and people. In this tiny Hong Kong apartment, the food-loving owners have allocated an area big enough for four people to have an intimate meal. A curved high-backed cane sofa seats two and echoes the curves of the oval table. The galley kitchen can be seen through the service hatch, screened by a white blind at night. The mix of western and eastern food eaten here is reflected in the range of tableware, collected on travels in Asia and Europe. White makes an attractive background for most food, and combines well with the green and blue of the celadon soya dishes.

Opposite A selection of Chinese ceramic spoons in shades of white, blue and green varies sharply from the European notion of the perfectly matched dinner service: the confidence to mix and match, coordinating each new course with a different style of ceramic, is part of the art of the Asian table.

Following spread This monolithic rock sink now rests in a private house in Kyoto, Japan. Made by American-Japanese sculptor Isamu Noguchi, it came from a Kyoto tea school. The present owner somewhat sacrilegiously cut off part of the rock on the right to make it fit its new space. On a cedar wood draining board stand teapots and cups for everyday use. A traditional Japanese kitchen would run along the outside wall of the house, separate from the living quarters: this kitchen is unusual in being part of an open-plan dining/studio room. The stone floor — practical and easily sluiced down — is rather spartan during Japan's cool winter .

Left above *Faux ivory chopsticks rest on a 1950s' Chinese ceramic 'baby', a symbol of prosperity (most elements in Chinese culture have a symbolic meaning. Three of the most common themes are prosperity, happiness and longevity). The chocolate and cream silk fabric is from Thailand.*

Left below *These gilded porcelain dishes were designed by Hong Kong-based, American artists Brad Davis and Janis Provisor, based on their paintings and drawings of Chinese natural forms. Following the tradition of Chinese landscape painting, the artists have taken their inspiration from the texture of trees, mountains and water, translating them into abstract eastern patterns.*

Right *In this Bangkok dining room, owner Lindsey Bailey has combined furniture and objects from the Philippines and Thailand to create a room that is light and informal during the day, but can be dressed up for an evening dinner party with ease. The early twentieth-century molave wood table is from the Philippines, as are the chairs, which have been covered in loose white cotton canvas. On a Spanish-style reproduction side-table in narra wood, also Philippine, stand a European art deco coffee set and a simple arrangement of twisted willow beneath a Thai beaten brass mirror. The windows are hung with a single layer of rich bronze raw silk from Jim Thompson Silk in Bangkok.*

Previous spread *Blue and white always make a strong combination, especially in ceramics.*

From left to right *1 Crackle-glaze duck-egg blue soya sauce dishes. 2 A Chinese chopper hangs with Western stainless-steel equipment against a background of deep blue formica. 3 Hand-painted Chinese porcelain spoons. 4 Textured lacquered wood Japanese bowls in black and oxblood. 5 Graphic calligraphy on a ceramic sake cup. 6 A stack of everyday Chinese plates with hand-painted fish motif. 7 Whisk of bleached twigs tied with metal twine. 8 Porcelain Chinese wine cups.*

Left *So passionate about food is the owner of this Bangkok house that he has built a separate pavilion for cooking. Exceptionally light, with glazed walls and high ceilings, this room relies on air-conditioning to make it practical during the day. With open shelves, white tiling, wood surfaces and a dining table for ten, it is welcoming in the tradition of the country-style kitchen. Displayed on high shelves is a collection of Thai, Ban Chieng pots, mixed among the hanging pans are local bean pods, while interspersed with the blue and white china and enamelware on the table are dried red chillies.*

Left *Chinese pottery, some made at the time of the Han dynasty (206BC–AD220) can be found throughout Southeast Asia. The style of this imported pottery influenced the evolution of ceramics both in this region and in northern Asia. Most of these pieces were 'export-ware', and of lesser quality than the pieces made for the royal court. Dispersed throughout Asia by traders, state missions and pilgrims, they were used for trade or as gifts. These porcelain dishes are 500 years old.*

Opposite above *Although first introduced to Europe in the early seventeenth century, tea has been known to Chinese botanists and the medical profession since the earliest of times. It can be prepared in many different ways and each region has its own time-honoured customs and practices. On the Indian sub-continent it is traditionally sweetened with a dash of condensed milk and sugar and known as cha; in China, black jasmine tea accompanies every meal, when it is poured haphazardly into small cups and onto the table alike; in Japan, the tea ceremony has been elevated to the status of an esoteric religion, in a ritual celebration of the mundane. The two bamboo-handled tea pots shown here are Japanese.*

Opposite below *The Japanese recognize that an imperfectly thrown pot can sometimes simultaneously be a perfect pot, while an unevenly applied glaze or brush stroke of oxide can mean the difference between decoration and art, defining this as 'the way of the clay'. This set of sake pot and cups is Korean, some 300 years old, displayed on a wooden dish which is also Korean and about 200 years old. The grey, putty tones of the glaze are freely painted on the pots' surface, bringing each hand-thrown object to life.*

Right *This contemporary Japanese 'slab pot' is constructed, rather than thrown, from flattened, rolled out pieces of clay. The square shape would be ideal for serving either sushi or a pile of fine, cold green soba noodles. An ingenious ledge for resting chopsticks has been built into the corners of the dish, adding to its graphic appeal.*

Opposite *Fire is the element of transformation, turning sand into ceramic or glass, and making metal malleable and workable. The intricately detailed and embossed pattern on these Chinese silver and ebony chopsticks adds a strong note of decorative contrast when used in conjunction with a plain, elegant table setting in a range of neutral tones.*

Right above *In the flexible space of this partially covered courtyard verandah in the Sri Lankan home of architect Anjalendran, stone and terracotta are the two predominant materials: red gravel with inset stones, smooth flagstone floors, rough stone walls and a terracotta tiled roof. These textures are offset by a large, practical wood table, which serves the dual function of acting as office space by day and converting to an area in which to entertain in the evening. Two unusual metal stools, resembling cloths hanging over raised boxes, and a metal sculpture on the table, add further textural variety to the setting.*

Right *In Thailand, cutlery is used rather than chopsticks, although it usually consists of forks and spoons only, with no knives. These Thai-made stainless steel, hollow-handled spoons, reassuringly sturdy and heavy in the hand, are extremely popular. Their rough/smooth finish works well with other textures, such as the grain of this wood table and the beaten pattern of the deep metal bowls.*

Far right *The lids of these small gold-coloured metal boxes — the size of match boxes — are decorated with Chinese calligraphy.*

WATER

Previous spread *Making the most of a spectacular view of the South China Sea, this Hong Kong bathroom is all about water: the most private room in the house goes public to an audience of sea birds. From the inside, meanwhile, a huge floor-to-ceiling picture-window frames a serenely breathtaking view. The combination of extreme contemporary architecture by Mike Tonkin Associates, and imported European bathroom fittings creates a surreal environment, juxtaposing the mundane with the unexpected.*

Right *This tropical idyll in Bali is a world away from the urban bustle and modern skyline of Hong Kong. Part of the Begawan Giri that sprawls down the Ayung River gorge near Ubud, this landscaped pool is filled with holy water from a natural spring. Lying above the confluence of two rivers, the area is particularly auspicious according to the animist beliefs (the attribution of conscious life to natural objects or to nature itself) of the local people. The owner, Bradley Gardner, has created a manmade environment that melds seamlessly with the natural one, in a mammoth feat of landscape gardening.*

**W**ater is a symbol of purity in many cultures. Constantly changing, water can be dark, silent, still and oppressive, or light, vibrant, energetic and joyful. Although opposites, there are similarities between the elements of water and fire: imbued with cleansing and regenerative powers, both can also be uncontrollable, destructive and terrifying.

It is a primal human desire to live near water. To live with water is calming, soothing and meditative, but living near water today, or having water in your home, nevertheless implies status and prosperity. In order to sustain life, man is dependent on the availability of and easy access to fresh water, and all early settlements were built near to rivers, wells and springs. In Indonesia, the well is traditionally the first part of a Javanese compound to be built and ritual cleansings are performed to insure the site is free of unwelcome malevolent forces.

Water contributes to and defines the changing seasonal landscape of Asia. From the man-made rice fields that glisten with water, the sacred importance of springs, rivers, waterfalls and lakes, to the ocean and seashore, water is inextricably linked with living in Asia. In this chapter we see how water can be brought into exterior living environments through landscaping and swimming pools. We discover interiors that incorporate water features and the therapeutic properties associated with water into their design. We also look at bathing traditions and bathroom styles.

Waterside landscapes are rich, varied and desirable. It is arguably Hong Kong Island's spectacular natural landscape surrounded by water that lends the extra dynamic edge to this tiny but vibrant city. Today, views of the bustling harbour can only be glimpsed between towering skyscrapers, meanwhile, the southside looks out across the islands of the South China Sea, and is dotted with some of the most expensive real estate in the world. In contrast, the coast of Sri Lanka with its rocky outcrops, beaches and coconut groves, was always considered inferior to the land in the cool and fertile tea-growing hill country. Ironically, today the beachside property is the more valued real estate.

Indonesia and Sri Lanka, set in miles of open sea, have their coasts pounded by monsoon storms. The tropical idyll can be an unsettling place to live when the constant roar of the ocean fills the mind, and buildings are battered by the elements, imbued with the scent of the ocean and saturated with salt water.

Water is important to man in many ways, not least in our home environments. Visually, water lends an extra dimension to gardens, either moving, as in waterfalls and fountains, or still, as in pools and ponds. All Japanese gardens include water in their design, from the waterfalls and pools that perfectly emulate natural water formations, to the representation of rippling water in dry gravel creations. Even very small Japanese gardens include a hollowed out, stone, water-filled pot. Tropical gardens invariably incorporate water features, either natural or man-made, creating a lush and humid living environment. All traditional tropical houses are built within the context of the dominant monsoon climate. Large stone pots are placed beneath the eaves of Balinese houses to collect rainwater during torrential downpours. Water pools placed near to tropical homes help to cool breezes before they enter the house. Traditional Malay architecture features a horizontal wood crenelated 'rain dripper', which helps drain water off the pitched tiled roof.

Swimming pools are a modern means of introducing water into the home, and in Asia they range from the simple recreation of a natural bathing pool to the architecturally designed urban pool. The 'negative edge' pool, popularized by exclusive hotels, is a device that blends pool and natural environment seamlessly. This can be seen to dramatic effect when perched on a hillside, as the pool appears to drop away into the jungle.

Above *When water is combined with architecture, the interplay of fluid and solid planes adds an extra dimension, sometimes transforming a previously unremarkable building into an extraordinary one. This small, rectangular pool, set within a courtyard at The Villa in Sri Lanka, is enclosed on all four sides. The introduction of a square 'window' into the wall separating the pool from the coconut grove beyond allows the eye to travel from water to framed view and back again, creating an environment that is dramatic and enticing.*

When water is brought inside the home it creates continuity with the natural world, and introduces the calming and cleansing properties we associate with it. In Chinese cultures, when it is not possible to live by a body of water, water is introduced through pools and aquariums inside the home. Water around the home regulates humidity and purifies the air. In India, during the searingly hot months, grass screens called tatties are soaked with water and hung outside windows to cool incoming air.

Bathing is an important aspect of life in the East. In the West we wash primarily to get clean; it is a solitary, daily chore, while Asian bathing is an enjoyable, often communal affair. Even today, sarong-clad women can be seen washing together at dusk in Bali's mountain streams. Thailand's beaches are abandoned by tourists when the sun fades, but this is when local families arrive to enjoy the cooling water and night air.

Japanese people have long appreciated the relaxing and rejuvenating qualities of their country's volcanic springs. From the secretive sacred springs, to the public baths and bathing at home, the art of bathing in Japan combines a thorough pre-cleanse followed by a meditative soak. The Japanese soaking bath is shorter, wider and deeper than Western baths. The water covers a seated person to the shoulders, encouraging a sensation of weightlessness that aids relaxation. The ritual of bathing Japanese-style means that everyone who enters the bath is already clean, so the water can be used many times. Japanese traditional bathrooms combine natural materials, stone and wood, and care is given to place the room so that it has a view outside if possible.

Tropical bathrooms range from simple open-roofed shacks that are an adjunct to the house, to luxury contemporary interpretations, with marble terrazzo flooring, imported sanitaryware and hot water. The basic concept is often the best; a large ceramic water pot and a smaller vessel for scooping out water are all that is needed for a satisfying bucket bath. Some of the most luxurious bathrooms are in the colonial houses and maharajahs' palaces of India and Sri Lanka. Often the scale of the room creates the first impression of opulence, while natural light from windows adds more sensual indulgence. Cool materials can be used to great effect in a hot climate; marble becomes even more appealing, so too does concrete painted with glossy white paint.

Textural stone, wood, even concrete and burnished metal, take on an earthy quality in the modern Asian bathroom, contrasting with stark white sanitaryware. A teak ladder can be used to hang towels, while growing bamboo naturally creates 'hooks' perfect for hanging loofahs. Soaps can be stored in clam shells, pots hewn from lava stone, even displayed on waxy leaves.

We have an instinctive yearning to surround ourselves with the soothing, healing properties of water. Looking to the East we should learn to take time to enjoy the simple pleasure of bathing.

Above *This urban pool in Singapore is overlooked by houses on all sides. The architect, Ernesto Bedmar, has solved the problem by creating an intimate walled private space, while avoiding any feeling of claustrophobia. Strategically placed 'windows' in a high whitewashed wall make the most of neighbours' gardens, framing dense tropical foliage while blocking out views of the building beyond. The clear lines of the stairway add more architectural definition, while the presence of a red-flowering hibiscus tree and Chinese ceramic pots place the house in its Asian context.*

Previous spread *In Asia there is a clear connection between how and where people live and the available water supply, while the Chinese belief in Feng Shui imbues water with powerful symbolic meaning.*

From left to right *1 Giant clam shells worn away by the ocean and scorched by the sun. 2 Feet and fresh water pummel yarn in a cotton-weaving factory in Sri Lanka. 3 A pool in a Japanese garden filled by a hollow bamboo conduit. 4 The weathered beams of a traditional teak house, up-ended and displayed like pieces of sculpture. 5 Stems of deep-green 'snake grass' or 'horse's tail'. 6 A Singapore swimming pool, where blue tiles contrast with shards of broken grey stones. 7 Ornamental koi carp swim in a Japanese garden. 8 In Singapore, a series of raised stone conduits feeds fresh water to a pool.*

Left *This Sri Lankan villa has a small garden surrounded by high laurel hedges. From the pillared verandah the garden reaches down in a series of wide red brick steps, lawn and frangipani trees to frame the classically inspired pool and fountain, transforming an otherwise limited view into a dramatic design statement.*

Above *This Singaporean shop-house has been opened up to provide as much cross-ventilation and natural light as possible. While keeping much of the original colonial architectural detail, such as the filigree door vents, the owner has injected a contemporary accent by using stone and polished marble and by keeping the walls and paintwork monochromatic. The sunken pool adds unexpected visual impact to the space. It also cools the air passing over it.*

The beauty of this bathroom lies in its combination of simplicity and a sense of low-key opulence. Lying on the ground floor of a colonial villa in Sri Lanka, it is constructed of concrete, plaster and tiling, and has a feeling of generous solidity and permanence. Though not over-large, it is none the less spacious, with lots of natural light shielded by cotton blinds which have a simple hook device to raise and lower them. The curves of a low dividing wall echo the vaulted ceiling and complement the filigree window vents, while the toilet, washbasin and bath are permanently built into the whitewashed concrete, giving the impression that the room has been like this for decades. Black skirting boards and simple wooden floor grates by the bath and washbasin add definition to the whiteness, which is practical and very easy to keep clean. The washbasin area has a triptych of two mirrors and a central window which provides an enchanting view.

Opposite *In Bali, the home of John and Cynthia Hardy is the culmination of a lifelong dream to build a house made completely from wood. In the pursuit of this unusual goal, they have made no sacrifice to comfort or convenience on any level. The master bathroom is arguably the pièce de résistance of the house. Raised on tall ironwood poles, it is situated on the living level of the house, while windows on all sides allow it to be opened out to the elements and afford stunning views of the rice terraces, rainforest and gorge of Sian Terrace. A combination of imported sanitaryware and a quirky use of materials – wood, bamboo and burnished copper – make this bathroom a luxurious folly. While the European bath is the height of indulgence, the burnished copper washbasin set in hardwood, the knobbly wood balustrade and the merbau wood floor keep the atmosphere earthy and appropriate for the jungle environment. Muslin drapes add to the romantic, old fashioned feeling of the bathroom as a whole.*

Right *A power-shower with an oversized copper shower-head pours onto a circular base of solid wood, made from a salvaged tabletop. The cubicle is spacious enough to make shower curtains or glass doors unnecessary, and is lined with panels of battered and burnished copper, which in time will change from brown to green. To the right is a corridor of closets with bamboo doors, and a Tibetan rug adds a touch of colour.*

Right *In Japan, baths have only one use — relaxation. A whole culture has grown up around the art of bathing, with venues varying from natural hot springs known only to the initiated, to traditional bathing houses, or onsen, and of course the domestic bathroom. Open-air baths are known as* roten buro. *Within the context of Japanese culture, which on the surface appears private and demure, communal bathing seems an anomaly to the outsider. Nevertheless, it is an extremely popular pastime. This rectangular onsen at Gora Kodan, a modern hotel built around natural hot springs in the foothills of Mount Fuji, is for men only. The architect, Kiyoshi Sey Takeyama, has employed straight lines to echo the dramatic angular stone landscaping outside. The separate women's pool is circular, and the arrangement and choice of stones and plants around the outside spring are more sensual, soft and curvaceous. These simple differences are an effective and instinctive way of defining the two spaces.*

Right and far right *Traditional bathrooms are becoming increasingly rare in Japan. Most people live in modern apartments where space is a luxury. But while the cypress tub may be fast disappearing, the arrangement of separate shower and bathing tub still exists, albeit often in formed plastic. This bathroom in Tokyo is a contemporary variation on the traditional bathroom. The first stage in having a bath, Japanese style, is to ensure that you are completely clean before you get into it. This is done sitting down, nowadays using a flexible shower hose, while the traditional water tub can be used to give a good head-to-toe dousing with water. After meticulous scrubbing with a cotton cloth and soap, followed by showering, the bather is ready to enter the bath. The cypresswood tub, or ofuro, (far right) is filled to the brim with piping hot water. The planks (on the left edge) are then placed across the box to keep the heat in while showering. In this way it is possible for the whole family to use the bath, one after the other, without the water getting too cold, and avoiding the need for complete refilling.*

Left *This austere tub in Singapore, by architects Kerry Hill Associates, is a new take on the traditional Japanese bath. Made of cast black concrete, it stands monumentally in the centre of the palest blue, light-filled room.*

Left *A wall, placed in the centre of this Bangkok bathroom, with the bath to one side and toilet on the other, encourages circular movement through the space, paralleling the Thai tradition of placing beds or furniture in the middle of rooms. This bathroom is an intelligent combination of thoughtful planning and low-cost finishes, elevated by a few well-chosen Asian antiques and Philippe Starck designed sanitaryware. The deep, angular bath is constructed of grey unpolished Thai marble. All the walls are plain whitewashed concrete except for the far wall, the texture of which was a happy accident — the result of removing a layer of mosaic tiles, which left a stubborn grey surface of hardened glue behind.*

Far left *A row of three square windows lets copious amounts of light into this pure white bathroom while creating a broken vista at eye-level. Towels and soaps are held at arm's reach on a spray-painted metal table designed by the owner, Jutti Subabhundit.*

Right *The bathroom is reached from the studio bedroom by a pair of 'temple doors', powder-coated matt white. Above the door, etched in the concrete, is the word 'bathroom' in Thai calligraphy. The dressing room and extra bedroom are announced in the same fashion. In the foreground is a bamboo opium mat, which is cool to the touch and would originally have lain on a raised opium bed. The object resembling a primitive space rocket is a Rajasthani papier-mâché storage box. Originally painted in earth colours, the owner painted it white to fit in with the modern Asian theme running through the whole apartment.*

Previous spread *The introduction of natural materials, even in cool functional bathrooms, helps to create a sensual, tactile bathing environment.*

From left to right *1 A loofah with a bamboo handle hangs against a solid wall of turquoise glass mosaic tiles. 2 Driftwood, shells and pods make an intriguing marine display. 3 This small washbasin is carved out of a single piece of wood, with a contrasting wood surround. 4 Loofahs, sponges, brushes and a mirror hang from a bamboo rail. 5 This unique table is made from salvaged wood. 6 Rounds of pure white soap and smooth stones rest on waxy leaves. 7 In an outside bathroom in Thailand, a towel rail is made from a piece of bleached driftwood. 8 A thin cotton cloth and a bar of soap in a Japanese bathroom.*

Left *One of life's simple luxuries in a tropical climate is bathing outdoors. Taking a cold shower in bright sunshine or under luminous stars is a far more invigorating and pleasurable experience than doing the same thing indoors. Here an ordinary shower attachment has been amusingly incorporated into this Balinese outdoor bathroom. Lost among ferns, orchids and tropical foliage, it becomes an extension of the stone sculptured wall. A carved head is incorporated into the rocky surround just above head height, benevolently watching over the bather, while a stone ledge provides a neat place for storing toiletries.*

Left and above *This simple outdoor bathroom in Thailand is attached to the house of a Buddhist monk. The bathing experience, with no concession to artifice, consists of cold water from a wall tap. Nevertheless, the combination of rough wood and textured plaster in the sunlight provides an appealing image of tropical living.*

Left *All the elements combine under a hot, tropical sun to create this vision of paradise in Bali. Begawan Giri sits in perfect harmony with the monsoon rainforest and paddy-fields of the sacred Ayung River gorge. Constructed of local paras stone, hardwoods, bamboo and grass thatch, the building melds with the natural environment and echoes the lines of traditional Balinese architecture. The mellow stone used for the walls creates a subtle patchwork effect and glows warmly in the sunlight. The swimming pool lined with rough green slate seems to fall away from the hillside to the jungle below, while the sounds and smells of the forest suffuse the atmosphere.*

Opposite *The raw coastline of Sri Lanka is treacherous for much of the year, encrusted with rock and coral reef, and pounded by waves that have travelled north for thousands of miles from the icy waters of the Antarctic. Here, however, it is captured during a serene and becalmed moment. Claughton, built on the southern tip of the teardrop-shaped island, enjoys spectacular views of a sweeping curved bay. The sun-scorched hillside, dotted with palms, descends gently to a steep rock-face where it meets the sea; while the pool cuts into the dramatic natural landscape with sharp, geometric precision.*

Alan Cleaver & Keith Varty, Thailand p. 72 (7)

Alison Henry Design Hong Kong/Thailand pp. 114, 115

Anjalendran, Sri Lanka pp. 5, 61, 115

Amanjiwo, Java pp. 68, 72 (6)

Barefoot, Sri Lanka pp. 72 (3), 122 (2)

Begawan Giri, Bradley Gardner, architect Yew Kuan Cheong, Bali
pp. 118, 140

Brad Davis & Janis Provisor, Fort Street Studio, Hong
Kong pp. 39, 84 (3), 84 (6), 106

Brief Gardens, Sri Lanka p. 32

Claughton, Sri Lanka pp. 5, 29, 56/57, 64, 141

Debra Little, Hong Kong, pp. 34 (5), 34 (7), 36/37,
84 (4), 101, 136 (2)

Douglas Johnson, Sri Lanka, pp. 51, 54 (2)

Douglas Young, G.O.D. Ltd. Hong Kong, pp. 34 (2),
74/75, 84 (8), 103, 108 (3),
108 (8), 112, 113

Ernesto Bedmar , Bedmar & Shi Designers, Singapore
pp. 22, 23, 53, 121, 122 (6), 122 (8)

Fu-Ka, Kobori Shuichiro, Japan, pp. 14/15, 28, 71,
94, 104/105, 136 (3)

Gerald Pierce, Thailand pp. 4, 110/111

Gora Kodan, Miwako Fujimoto, Japan pp. 52, 63,
76, 122 (5), 130/131

Jean-Francois Fauchet, Bali, p. 138

Jérôme Abel Seguin, Sumbawa, pp. 20 (7), 23 top
34 (6), 38, 41, 47, 60, 66/67,
80/81, 98 (2), 108 (6), 122 (1), 122 (4)

Jutti Supabhundit, Gote Design, Thailand, pp. 13,
34 (1), 91, 98 (5), 134/135

John & Cynthia Hardy, architect Yew Kuan Cheong, Bali,
pp. 42/43,65, 98 (7), 128/129, 136 (4), 136 (5),

John & Lee Lightbody, Thailand, pp. 44, 54 (7)

Kaoru Watanabe, Japan pp. 20 (4), 33, 88, 98 (4), 97,
112

Kimlan Cook, Japan, pp. 133, 136 (8)

Kondaya Genbei Co., Emi Yamaguchi, Japan, pp. 26,
34 (4), 40, 62, 82, 84 (5), 122 (3)

Kyoko Chirathivat, Thailand, pp. 8/9, 24/25, 27,
87

The Lee House, Peter Lee, Justin Hill, Kerry Hill Architects,
Singapore, pp. 19, 20 (6), 101, 132,
136 (1)

Lindsey & Geoff Bailey, Thailand pp. 86, 89, 107

Louise Ku, Hong Kong, pp. 72 (4), 72 (8), 98 (1)

Michael Chiang, Richard Ho Architects, Singapore,
pp. 20 (8), 125

Mike Tonkin & Anna Liu pp. 30/31, 102, 108 (1),
108:(2), 108 (4), 108 (5), 108 (7)

Michael Chan, Tonkin Architects London & Hong Kong,
pp. 92/93, 116/117

Muang Kula Pan, Thailand pp. 54 (4), 54 (5), 54 (8),
72 (2), 84 (2), 90, 98 (3), 98 (6), 98 (8),
136 (6), 136 (7), 139

Pia Pierre, Thailand, p. 34 (8)

Robert Champagne, 01 Architects, Hong Kong, p. 34 (3)

Soo Khian Chan, SCDA Architects, Singapore, pp. 16,
18, 20 (2)

Sopitsuda Maivun, Thailand, p. 54 (1)

Sun House, Sri Lanka, pp. 2, 20 (5), 28, 51,
78/79, 96, 124

Takashi Inaba, Bali, pp. 41, 70, 83

The Villa, Sri Lanka, pp. 20 (1), 20 (3), 54 (6), 58/59
120, 126/127

Way Man Sing, Hong Kong, p. 3

Walter & Hinke Zieck, p. 100

Warwick Purser, Out of Asia, Java, pp. 6, 77

In addition to the people listed above, who kindly allowed us into
their lives, we would also like to thank those who have generously
given their time and advice, an occasional bed for the night, or a
good meal and entertaining company. Without their help our job
would have been much more difficult, and much less fun. A big
thank you to:

Hong Kong – Sophie & Simon Walker, especially Sophie, who has
been a great friend, travel buddy and colleague over the years;
Sharon Leece, Rachel Leedham and Christine Ho at *Elle Decoration*;
Amanda Dick; Mike Tonkin & Anna Liu; Douglas Young at G.O.D.
Indonesia – Olivia & Francois Richli at Amanjiwo; Warwick Purser
& Amier at Out of Asia; Julia Gajcak, Royal & Pamela Rowe at The
Four Seasons, Bali; Aulia; Jérôme Abel Seguin; Emily Readett-
Bailey; Linley; Bradley Gardiner; Cheong Yew Kuan; Michelle Han;
Made Wijaya.
Japan – Rumiko Fujioka; Astrid Klein & Mark Dytham at Klein
Dytham Architects; Teruo Kurosaki at Idee; Miwako Fujimoto at
Gora Kadan; Gaynor Stevens; Toyozumi Nonoyama & Masaichi
Tamaoki at *Elle Decoration*.
Singapore - Kate & Askandar Samad; Soo Khian & Lorretta Chan;
Emma Douglas-Hamilton; Christina Ong.
Sri Lanka – Mary McIntyre & Joel Pauleau at Sun House, Jed &
Mayquai Donahoe; Ernest at The Villa, Anjelendran; Charles Hulse;
Douglas Johnson; Jessica Langton; Domenic & Nazareen Sansoni.
Thailand – Charlotte Bevan & Jim Williams; Andy & Andrea
Stevens; Keith Varty & Alan Cleaver; Rungsima Kasikranund at *Elle
Decoration*; Gilles Caffier.

Quotes

pg 18 Tadao Ando quote taken from *From the Row House in
Sumiyoshi to the Town House in Kujo*, Shinkenchiku, July 1983.
pg 18 William Lim quote taken from an article by Elizabeth Gwee
in *The Straits Times*, October 1997.
pg 19 Loius Khan quote taken from *Light is The Theme*, Louis I
Kahn and The Kimbell Art Museum, 1975.